HOMETOWN HUMOR, U.S.A.

PRAISE FOR

Loyal Jones & Billy Edd Wheeler

Laughter in Appalachia

"A delightful, giggle-a-minute collection of yarns told simply and
eloquently by mountain folks for whom humor is a way of life."
—SOUTHERN LIVING

"Laughter pealing from the mountains."
—INDIANAPOLIS NEWS

"We need to laugh more and this book is a way to do it. We owe
Loyal and Billy Edd a large thank you for putting this collection
together."
—ASHVILLE CITIZEN-TIMES

"The real stuff . . . with authentic roots."
—GREENVILLE (S.C.) NEWS

"Sometimes the humor is as ancient as the Bible, and sometimes it
is as
up-to-date as the morning paper."
—LOUISVILLE COURIER-JOURNAL

Curing the Cross-Eyed Mule

"You're going to love this book. It's funny, really funny."
—CHET ATKINS, C.G.P.

"The book's appeal is diverse, reaching far beyond mere regional interest."
—BOOKLIST

"*Curing the Cross-Eyed Mule* is a bellybuster."
—JAMES STILL

"A side-splitter . . . the two have put enough ammunition together to keep a laughter machine firing like a machine gun."
—CHATTANOOGA TIMES

"The joke thieves are at it again, and nothing is sacred . . . Jones's autobiographical sketch tells more about Appalachian people than a ton of statistics."
—LOUISVILLE COURIER-JOURNAL

HOMETOWN HUMOR, U.S.A.

*Over 300 jokes and stories from the
porch swings, barber shops, corner cafés,
and beauty parlors of America.*

Loyal Jones and
Billy Edd Wheeler

August House Publishers, Inc.
LITTLE ROCK

Printed in the United States of America

10 9 8 7 6 5 4 3 2

LIBRARY OF CONGRESS CATALOGING-IN-PUBLICATION DATA

Hometown humor, USA : more than 300 jokes from the porch swings,
barber shops, corner cafés, and beauty parlors of America / [edited by]
Loyal Jones and Billy Edd Wheeler — 1st ed.
p.   cm.

ISBN 0-87483-139-3 (hardback : acid-free) : $19.95
ISBN 0-87483-138-5 (paperback : acid-free) : $9.95
1. American wit and humor.
2. United States—Social life and customs—1971- —Humor.
I. Jones, Loyal, 1928- .   II. Wheeler, Billy Edd.
PN6162.h645 1991
818'.540208—dc20   91-22794

Note: "Snuff Dipper" and the other comedy material from Mike Snider is
copyrighted by Woodrich Pub. Co. (BMI) and used here by permission. To
order Mike Snider/Live on the Boat and other LPs and cassettes, write Mike
Snider, Banjo Picker, Gleason, TN 38229.

Executive: Liz Parkhurst
Project editor: Judith Faust
Design director: Ted Parkhurst
Cover design: Kitty Harvill, Harvill–Ross Studios
Typography: Lettergraphics, Little Rock

This book is printed on archival-quality paper which meets the
guidelines for performance and durability of the Committee on
Production Guidelines for Book Longevity of the
Council on Library Resources.

AUGUST HOUSE, INC.   PUBLISHERS   LITTLE ROCK

*For all you characters
who have made our hometowns
laughable... uh... we mean "memorable,"
and for all our neighbors, far and near,
who have made us laugh*

Preface

This book results from our long pursuit of humor and, of course, from the last two books we did together with August House: *Laughter in Appalachia: A Festival of Southern Mountain Humor* (1987) and *Curing the Cross-Eyed Mule: Appalachian Mountain Humor* (1989). These books proved what we already knew: that people crave a good laugh, and that they will go to great lengths to get it, even so far as to buy a book.

All kinds of people from all around the country have written us to say how much they enjoyed these books—and better yet, to send us their favorite stories in the hope we would do another book. So that's what we have done. Ted Parkhurst at August House suggested we do something that would reach beyond our native region of Appalachia, reflecting the humor of rural and small-town America.

You who have read the other two books know that we did humor festivals at Berea College in Berea, Kentucky, both to highlight humor and to give people a chance to share their best stories with us. We decided to do a third festival during the summer of 1990, and it was just as much fun as the first two. We invited some funny and entertaining people: Joe Bly, an Asheville, North Carolina, humorist and motivational speaker; Ramona and Alisa Jones from Nashville, who have appeared at the Grand Ole Opry and on "Hee Haw," and who brought along Ruth McLain Smith and Larry Sledge; Bob Hannah, an Atlanta movie and TV actor and storyteller; Paul Lepp and Bonnie Collins, West Virginia storytellers and humorists; and Dr. Bill Foster, from Florence, Alabama, an English teacher who plays the banjo, sings good songs, and tells fine stories.

People came from all over the place to listen and to participate in the contests we devised. We collected some great stories in the festival, and they are in this book. We thank all those listed above and all the others for their stories.

We also invited two scholars who have reflected on and studied the importance of humor to health and healing. They are Dr. John Combs, professor of English at Kentucky Wesleyan College in Owensboro, and Dr. Michael R. Nichols, director of the Counseling Center at the University of Kentucky and a teacher in the College of Medicine. They not only said important things about humor and health, they were funny, too. Their speeches are included in this collection. They make sense to us, since we believe rural and small-town people have kept a better perspective on life than some others who are caught up in various rat races in some of the overgrown metropolitan areas, *and* we believe a humorous outlook may have something to do with that perspective.

We have continued to collect stuff on our own, and each of us wrote to our friends for stories, or made friends with those who had good ones. We thank all of you who sent us or told us stories, especially Chet Atkins, C.G.P.; Tom T. Hall; Mike Snider; Margaret and Richard Bailey; John Ed McConnell; Dr. Carl Hurley; Judge Ray Corns; Sarah Ophelia Cannon (a.k.a. Minnie Pearl); John Ferguson; Ed Ward; Katie Letcher Lyle; Judge Sam J. Ervin, III for permission to use a few stories from his late father, Senator Sam J. Ervin, Jr.; and Sammy Ford and Kentucky State Senator Danny Ford for permission to use stories from their grandfather, the late Charles Carter. We especially want to thank the children at the Clinton County Elementary School in Albany, Kentucky—Willie Aaron, Charnett Patton, Ami Cravens, Pamela

Looper, Dana McFall, Tonya Marcum, Martina Burchett, Beth Stearns and April Stinson—for contributing stories when we visited the school. We appreciate you all, and we apologize if we've failed to give anyone credit. In a few cases, we have long forgotten who told us a particular story or we have lost our notes.

Finally, we'd like to thank our new editor, Judith Faust, for her help in grouping these jokes and stories, coming up with imaginative titles for them, and well, for her overall creative touch in shaping the book into what it is.

We hope you enjoy this book as much as we have enjoyed doing it. Please let us know if you do—or even if you don't! Send us your favorite story if it's not in here. You never saw anyone who enjoys such gifts more than we do.

Billy Edd Wheeler
P.O. BOX 7
SWANNANOA, NORTH CAROLINA

Loyal Jones
111 FOREST STREET
BEREA, KENTUCKY

Contents

My Hometown

LOYAL JONES

The wit makes fun of other persons; the satirist makes fun of the world; the humorist makes fun of himself, but in so doing, he identifies himself with other people—that is, people everywhere, not for the purpose of taking them apart, but simply revealing their true nature.

James Thurber

The oral tradition is said to be in bad shape, what with TV, video movies, endless sports events, and other stuff more threatening to the human race. In 1973, some characters seeming to be of a mind that yarn-spinners are going the way of the passenger pigeon got together in Jonesborough, Tennessee, and started the National Association for the Preservation and Perpetuation of Storytelling. Other similar enterprises emerged, such as The Corn Island Storytelling Festival over in Louisville. I applaud these efforts because they keep the perpetrators out of other kinds of trouble and because the folks who organized them are pretty near right about the oral tradition.

I agree you don't hear many folk or fairy tales on the street or back porch any more—maybe because everybody's in too big of a hurry to listen that long—but I find that folks still take time to tell (and listen to) stories with a punch line

13

that tickles them a little bit. My hometown of Berea, Kentucky, is a fine place to hear these kinds of stories.

Come along while I amble around. There's Dr. Charles Harris. He's a retired physician who looks more like Fred MacMurray than Fred MacMurray does. He's grinning, so he has a story...

> *Did you hear the one about this fellow who was driving down the road in his car going maybe sixty-five, and this chicken passed him? Well, it looked like it had three legs, but he wasn't sure. It turned into a driveway and disappeared behind this house. A man was sitting on the front porch, so he threw on his brakes, skidded to a stop, and asked, "Did that chicken have three legs?"*
>
> *"Yes," the man said. "We bred them for Kentucky Fried Chicken."*
>
> *"Well," said the other fellow, "I bet you've made a fortune."*
>
> *"No," said the man. "We ain't been able to catch one yet."*

Here comes Hilda Woodie. She's a schoolteacher, which doesn't keep her from talking like Minnie Pearl when she tells a story. She doesn't waste any time...

> *An education-conscious man saw this little boy loafing along the road on a schoolday.*
>
> *"Aren't you going to school?" he asked.*
>
> *"Nope."*
>
> *"Why not?" he persisted.*
>
> *The boy said, "We busted the basketball."*

The school-improvement people might well take note of that story, but never mind, there's Billy Wilson. He ran the shoe-repair shop in town before he decided to retire and start fishing full-time. He's grinning, too...

> *I haven't told you this one. Back in the days when people rode the buses all day, they'd take picnic baskets*

and put them up on the luggage racks above their heads. The men traveling alone would look to see where the picnic baskets were so as to try to get a free meal. A man got on this bus, saw a big basket, and sat down under it next to a lady. Soon he felt something dripping on his face.

He licked his lips and asked, "Pickles, ma'am?"

"No. Pups," she answered.

It's good to see Dr. Louis Smith. He is the retired dean of Berea College, an erudite scholar who has kept a lot of the flavor of his native Middle Tennessee…

Did I tell you this one about Governor Bob Taylor of Tennessee when he was a boy? His father got exasperated with him one day because of his stubbornness.

"You are a mule, Bob, a mule," he said and walked off.

When he was almost out of hearing, Bob called after him, "Daddy, if I am a mule, what does that make you?"

I need a haircut, and at Melvin Higgins's place you get more than a trim—like the latest in underground news and an assessment of the jumbled political scene. He is a whole lot better barber than this story indicates…

A man came in here, got up into the chair, said, "Now, I want you to cut this sideburn off here even with the top of my ear, and this other one down here level with my earlobe. Then cut the hair real close on this side and leave it long on the other side."

I said, "I don't believe I can do that."

He said, "Well, I don't know why. That's how you did it the last time I came in here."

Don and Nancy Graham run a couple of craft shops uptown, and Don has also been a Disciples of Christ preacher for nearly thirty years. He is a genial Georgian, and he'd rather converse than eat—that and tell stories...

> *Did you hear about the woman of ninety-four who sued her husband for divorce? They'd celebrated their seventy-fifth anniversary and all. Well, somebody asked her why, if she was going to do it, she didn't do it earlier, and she said, "Well, I wanted to wait until all of the children had died."*

The wonderful thing about my hometown (and a lot of other towns I visit) is that there are plenty of people who can tell you entertaining and funny stories, and they range from college professors—and even presidents—to people who do real work for a living. No matter what station they hold or aspire to, they retain a vestige of the old oral tradition from a more rustic way of life. That quality ties us to the entire human enterprise with all its disappointments, surprises, and joys.

There is a whole lot more to it than just jokes. Telling and listening to these stories is a way to relate to one another in an age of increasing detachment, a way to enjoy and appreciate each other. Amiable relationships get harder in this electronic and internal combustion age when we go skittering about like weasels in a henlot. When we *do* come to rest, we most often make contact with one another electronically if at all. I'm not knocking conveniences. I do some skittering about myself in a Chevrolet Corsica, and I am writing this piece on a Macintosh, jiggling one leg up and down while I listen to Bill Malone's *Classic Country Music* (Smithsonian Collection) on my JVC boombox with Super Bass Horn.

In my heart, though, I'd rather be riding a horse, and I'd prefer sitting down for a long evening of talking with Bill Malone about Southern culture and country music than listening to tapes, or maybe even going with him to visit one of the survivors in his collection, such as Patsy Montana, Pee Wee King, or Tennessee Ernie Ford. They know something about the human condition and have talked and sung about human frailties, mistakes, and occasional heroics all their lives.

As we let technology and our lifestyles shut us off from easy and personal contact, we need to make a special effort to keep in touch with others. I believe jokes and stories are one way we enjoy each other and in the process also learn about all our human qualities. Jokes look simple and not very important, but if you look a little harder, they comment on our fears, our loves, and the truths that lie beneath our surface interactions.

The humor of jokes and funny stories is one of our great pleasures. We all crave laughter and seek it. Laughter makes us feel good and brings warmth and gratitude toward those who make us laugh. As the essays (later in the book) by John Combs and Mike Nichols affirm, laughter is good for us. It makes us feel better whether our trouble is emotional or physical. Norman Cousins and others have written much in recent years about humor and health and healing.

Humor is one of the best coping mechanisms in our relationships with others and in our own private travails with sickness and death. It brings perspective. It helps us to see that we are not the center of things—that God, or other people, have probably not picked us out exclusively to punish or embarrass. Humor helps us to take the wider view, to see ourselves properly in relation to others. It helps us accept ourselves and others and see both us and them more realistically. Through humor, we mature; we gain the integrity (the integration of all our parts, experiences, dreams, and accomplishments) that enables us to face life with all of its pleasures and all of its sorrows. Humor is our best friend.

Every day when I walk to work, I keep a lookout for my friends who know I crave a laugh and who will oblige me, and I try to have one for them. I'm sort of like Zebulon Vance of North Carolina in Civil War times, who when he campaigned for office would take along a little packet of beans. He would tell the lady of the first house he visited that his wife had sent her a few beans for a start and she wondered if the lady would give her some of her variety of beans. The lady would fix up a batch, and off he'd go to the next house, saying the new packet was the beans his wife had fixed. Thus he always had a packet to give away.

I pick up jokes and stories that way, pass them on, and expect one in return to share with someone else. It is a pretty good racket, especially if people buy this book.

Tickling the Hog's Back

B I L L Y   E D D   W H E E L E R

I am intimidated by big places and big events: the razzle-dazzle of the Super Bowl, hyped by glamorous people and glittering graphics, with music that seems to be announcing the Second Coming; international airports with moving sidewalks, electronic signs, and computer voices; New York City with its towering skyline, the noisy bustle of its millions, the gleam of brass and gold and glass.

I think, where do I fit into all this?

I feel small and unimportant. Insignificant.

Then I remember what makes the Super Bowl interesting: people. Sore ankles, weak knees, a busted thumb...little details about people made of flesh and blood...like me. People from hometowns like mine.

The same with airports. People coming and going from hometowns around the world, laughing and crying, saying hello and goodbye.

The same with New York City. People living in their hometown *within* the city, their four square blocks where they live out their lives in a corner of the borough, their neighborhood with its drugstore, barber shop, deli, supermarket, dance hall, furniture store. People gossiping about their friends, telling jokes and stories...

> *Did you hear about Freddie, our local furniture salesman? He finally got a date with a nice looking lady. Can you believe it, our Freddie, out on the town with a real looker?*
>
> *The only problem is, he goes to pick her up and finds that she has a severe case of laryngitis or some-thing...she can't talk. She can't even whisper. But Fred-die is trying, right? He's making conversation, using sign language, all kinds of stuff.*
>
> *Finally he says, "So what would you like to do?"*
>
> *She draws a picture of a steak. Freddie gets the idea and takes her to a nice steak place and they have a wonderful meal.*
>
> *Then Freddie says again, "So what would you like to do now?"*
>
> *She draws a picture of an ice cream cone. So he takes her to the dairy bar and they have a nice cone of cream.*
>
> *As he walks her home, he squeezes her hand and she squeezes his. And once again he says, "What would you like to do now?"*
>
> *She draws a picture of a bed.*
>
> *Freddie looks at her in amazement. Says, "How in the world did you know I was in the furniture business!"*

Green Beans and Fatback

I was born in a small town, raised in small towns, went to small high schools and even smaller colleges, so the in-timidation factor was still at work when I went off to Yale University to do graduate work in playwriting. I felt ignorant and insecure when I heard my classmates talking about current hits on Broadway. I had never seen a Broadway show.

But something happened in a playwriting class that helped me put things in perspective. We were told to write a short scene that dealt with a traumatic incident in our past, a scene with conflict and authentic details. So I wrote about burning a pot of beans when I was "batching it" with my grandfather, having run off from home, which was then Highcoal, West Virginia.

My Granddad dearly loved his green beans. He grew them in his own garden.

One day he told me to watch the beans while he was off working on the railroad. He gave me instructions: "Let the beans simmer for several hours. I like to cook 'em slow, with a piece of streaked meat (fatback) in there for seasoning. But you have to add water every now and again. So be sure and check on them. Don't let 'em burn."

Well, I was fourteen and loved football, and so did my buddies there in Eskdale, West Virginia. We didn't have a football; we used a tin can, usually a Carnation milk can, but we had fun playing just the same. So while the beans were cooking, we decided to choose up sides and play some tin can football, and we got carried away and forgot all about the beans.

Until I smelled them. Clear out in the yard.

In a terrified frenzy, I rushed inside and took the beans off the flame. The ones on the bottom were half black and stuck to the bottom of the pot. I got the bright idea of lifting off the unburned beans, scraping out the burned ones, putting the good beans back, with the fatback, and adding water. Maybe it would work. The beans looked fine.

But of course they weren't. My Granddad was so angry he made me go back home. This was too much. I'd played hooky, the truant officer had visited him several times, and I'd been into a lot of other trouble, but this was the last straw. Our batching days were over. I ended my scene with the observation, "You burn one bean, you burn them all!"

It was a simple scene, to say the least, but overnight, I was famous at Yale. Classmates would see me in the hall and yell out, "Hey, Wheeler, you burn one bean, you burn 'em all!" Second- and third-year playwriting students started coming around to my apartment offering to collaborate on scripts. For a while I was baffled. Then I slowly began to realize the value of hometown stories, authentic details, real-life characters, and phrases that have the ring of truth. Colorful stuff that you can't make up. You had to be there. Maybe that's why one of my first songs starts out like this:

I hope heaven's like the place where I come from.
Cows in the barn and time for a yarn
And work to make a living.
It's not the place where you'd get bored,
There's a fight now and then,
Fellow thinks he's the Lord.
But home is where the heart is
And my heart is heaven bound.
I hope heaven's just like my hometown.

Actually, I've had a lot of hometowns: Whitesville and Highcoal, West Virginia; Swannanoa, North Carolina; Berea, Kentucky; and Nashville, Tennessee. And I *feel* like I've lived in some towns that were made up: Garrison Keillor's Lake Wobegon, Thornton Wilder's Grover's Corners in his American classic, *Our Town*, and Andy Griffith's famous Mayberry, with Opie, Aunt Bea, Barney, and all the gang.

The things I remember about these real and made-up towns are the people who made me laugh. And cry. Telling stories. Making jokes even while talking about life and death.

An Early Riser

Elwood Suggins, in one of my hometowns, wasn't feeling too well, so he went to see the doctor. The doctor shocked him by telling him he had a rare disease that had already progressed to the point where nothing could be done. It was terminal.

"How much time do I have, Doc?" the man asked, and the doctor told him six hours!

22

So Elwood rushed home and told his wife the bad news. After they sat in sad silence for a few minutes, his wife asked him how he wanted to spend his last six hours. He told her he wanted to make love. So they made love for two hours.

"You've got four hours left, so what do you want to do now?" she asked him. He thought for a minute and decided he would like to make love again. So they made love for another two hours. After a minute or two, she asked him what he would like to do with his remaining two hours, and, once again, he said he would like to make love.

This time, their lovemaking lasted only an hour. Since he still had one hour left, he was thinking hard, trying to decide what he would like to do, when his wife said, "Look, honey, I'm beat. I'm really tired, so I think I'll go on to bed and get some sleep."

"Sleep!" Elwood yelled. "How can you even think about sleeping at a time like this? I want to do something. I sure don't want to go to bed and go to sleep."

"Yeah," the wife replied, "but you don't have to get up in the morning."

Sex Education

Of course, sex is a big topic in small towns, even if sex education is feared and frowned upon in many of them. I remember in one of my hometowns there was a hot debate about whether sex education should be taught in the third grade. At the PTA meeting, one parent stood up and very earnestly said, "I don't think I am opposed to sex education. We probably need it. But far as I'm concerned, eight is way too young to be calling things by their right names!"

An Unnatural Family Tree

A nine-year-old girl was working on an essay for school about her family origins, so at supper she decided to mix in a little research with the conversation. She asked her mother, "Mom, where did I come from?"

Her mother was an old-fashioned lady, so she said, "Well, honey, the stork brought you."

"Where did you come from, then?"

"Well, sugar, the stork brought me, too."

The little girl looked a little puzzled but continued. "OK, where did Grandpa and Grandma come from?"

"Uh, well, the stork brought them, too, dear."

She thanked her mother and settled down to writing her essay. A few minutes later, she took a break to watch TV, and her mother, curious to see what she had written, picked up her paper and read, "For three generations, there have been no natural births in our family."

Sex and Sailing

There's a small private school, Warren Wilson College, in my favorite hometown of Swannanoa, that several years ago had an enrollment of almost thirty percent foreign students. (Today it is closer to twenty percent.) With this wonderful international flavor, there was a colorful mix of cultures and traditions.

Once, the chairman of the board of trustees was asked by the president to give an informative talk to the entire student body. When he asked what his topic should be, the president said, "I think it would be most interesting to everyone, and especially enlightening to our foreign students, if you gave a talk about sex."

After some hesitation the chairman said he would do it and it was scheduled. But for some reason, when he got home and his wife asked him what he was going to talk about, he told her a little white lie, just to kid her, thinking he would tell her the truth later. He said, "I'm going to talk about sailing." Before he could set her straight, some company popped in and the conversation flowed to other subjects. He forgot about it.

24

He gave his talk on sex a few days later, and it went over so well, one of the staff saw his wife and remarked, "Say, your husband gave a great talk to the student body today!"

"That's funny," his wife said. "In fact, it's amazing. He's only done it three times. The first time, he got sick to his stomach. The second time, his hat blew off. And the third time, his foot got caught in the ropes, and he said, 'Never again!'"

A Difference in Anatomies

My naked three-year-old nephew sat in the bathtub with his cousin of the same age, who was also naked, and said to her as she stared at him, "Huh-uh, you can't play with mine. I'm afraid you'll lose it...like you did yours."

Expensive Birthday Present

Her birthday was coming up, so a husband asked his wife what sort of present she wanted, but she answered, "I really don't think I should say."

He said, "How about a diamond ring?" and she said she didn't care much for diamonds.

He said, "How about a mink coat?" and she reminded him that she didn't like furs.

"A gold necklace?" he suggested, but she declined, saying she already had several and didn't need another.

Finally he gave up and asked her what she did want.

"A divorce," she said. "That's what I'd really like."

Her husband hesitated only a minute and replied, "Well, I wasn't planning on spending quite that much!"

Hometown Stories

As you can see, it is hard to talk about hometown memories and values and people without telling stories. And I love to tell stories. Even in my songs, I am known as a *story*

25

songwriter. Fortunately for all of us, stories will always be in vogue.

And fortunately for me, I know a lot of wonderful storytellers personally. Not many of them *create* original stories, like Garrison Keillor, who is the greatest storyteller of all, but they love to pass them on. Chet Atkins does. He'll call me long distance to tell me a new joke or funny anecdote, and when he found out I was working on a new book with Loyal Jones, he started calling people like Minnie Pearl for me and bringing books by my place in Nashville. One absolute treasure he dropped off was his father's scrapbook, with old papers and letters and clippings dating back to the twenties, some written in his daddy's hand. His jokes are as funny today as they were then, and we've included some of them in another part of this book.

And there's Howard White of Neely's Bend Road in Madison, Tennessee, who is a fine joke teller and an even finer laugher. Howard's laugh is so free and infectious and quick to erupt, you can tell jokes with him for hours and not get tired.

Howard tells about one of his neighbors out there, Charlie Warren, who…

> …*was building a hog pen one day when another neighbor, a Mr. Holmes, dropped by and made an observation.*
>
> *"Charlie," he said, "that bottom board looks too high to me. It'll allow them hogs to get out."*
>
> *Charlie allowed that the board did look to be too high, but he said, "It is just low enough to scrape that hog's back as he goes out. And it'll feel so good to him, he'll turn around and come back in."*

A Right Strong Storm

> *Mr. Warren and Mr. Holmes got to talking about storms and Mr. Holmes said, "The worst one I ever saw was in 1939. The wind blew so hard, I saw a chicken lay the same egg three times. It blowed the kitchen out the*

back window, turned the tea kettle spout wrong-side-out, and got the days of the week so mixed up that Friday didn't get there until late Monday evening!"

Well, here I am again, telling stories given to me by friends, which is what *Hometown Humor, U.S.A.* is all about, I guess. I might as well stop pretending to write an essay about storytelling and just tell stories.

Dig in and help yourself. If you see a joke or something you like and want to be the first to tell it to one of your friends, why, just scooch under that bottom board there and run loose with it.

I hope it scrapes your funny bone and brings you back for more. 'Cause just like Charlie Warren's hogs, jokes are always coming and going, and they make you feel good either way.

"Then It Was Too Late"

C O U R T S H I P   A N D
M A R R I A G E

Widely Traveled

I haven't been in many states—the state of West Virginia, the state of Kentucky, the state of matrimony, and the state of ignorance. The last two are just the same.

Bonnie Collins
WEST UNION, WEST VIRGINIA

It Was Mutual

I speak at conventions, which is what I do for a living. I was in the lobby of one of these big hotels, and they have these big sofas back to back. I was sitting on one, and some people brought an older couple and put them on the couch behind me while they went for the car. They'd been celebrating their fiftieth wedding anniversary all afternoon and they were just about pooped out.

They didn't know I was there and I didn't want to intrude, so I sort of scrunched down on the sofa, and he said loudly, "Margaret?"

She said, "What?"

29

He said, "I'm proud of you!"
And she said "What?"
He said as loud as he could, "I'M PROUD OF YOU!"
She said, "THAT'S ALL RIGHT, HONEY. I'M TIRED
OF YOU TOO."

Joe Bly
ASHEVILLE, NORTH CAROLINA

Bliss

I didn't know what true happiness was until I got married. Then it was too late. My wife's cooking was so bad the flies got together to mend the screens.

Paul Kuczko
WISE, VIRGINIA

Logic

Somebody told my wife that I had been chasing women. She said, "So what? I've got a dog that chases cars, but he wouldn't know what to do with one if he caught it."

Manuel "Old Joe" Clark
RENFRO VALLEY, KENTUCKY

Perspective

"Was your wife mad when you got home so late last night?"
"Yes, she was plumb historical."
"Don't you mean hysterical?"
"No, historical. She brought up things that happened forty years ago."

The late Brooks Hays
LITTLE ROCK, ARKANSAS

That, or Restraint

A woman who had fourteen children was asked what quality she most admired in a man.
"Moderation," she said.

Loyal Jones

Another Prolific One

There was this other woman who had so many children she ran out of names to call her husband.

Minnie Pearl

NASHVILLE, TENNESSEE

Nothing's Surefire

A census taker came to call on a couple and asked how many children they had. The wife said, "Well, there was the first set of twins, Bill and Nell, and the second set, Thelma and Velma, and the third set, Lester and Vester..." The census taker interrupted to ask, "Did you always get twins?"

"No," the woman said, "sometimes we never got nothing."

Jim Rickels

MT. VERNON, KENTUCKY

Envying the Expert

A woman who had been married and divorced four times was invited by a friend to go hear a professor from the local college speak on love and marriage. She listened intently. Afterwards, her friend asked her what she thought of the lecture.

"Well," she said, "I wish I knew as little about the subject as he did."

Elwood Cornett

BLACKEY, KENTUCKY

Some Problem or Other

A census taker was interviewing a fellow who had a little trouble with his English.

"How many children do you have?" he asked.

"None, "the man said. "My wife is unbearable...I mean inconceivable...I mean impregnable."

Loyal Jones

31

Glad You Asked...

The minister's wife asked, "How did the wedding go?"

The minister said, "Fine until I asked the bride if she would obey, and she said, 'Do you think I'm crazy?' The bridegroom, who was in a sort of daze mumbled, 'I do.' Then things really started to happen."

Judge Ray Corns

FRANKFORT, KENTUCKY

Long Dry Spell

This married couple decided that they were too much interested in sex, so they decided that would make love only in the months that had an "R" in them. This worked all right until they went through May, June, and July.

One evening the man came in from work and asked, "What month is it?"

"Aurgust," his wife replied.

Billy Wilson

BEREA, KENTUCKY

Getting Repairs

A man came home from work pretty tired, and his wife asked him to fix the dishwasher. "Do I look like Mr. Fixit?" he said.

The next night he came home, and she asked him to fix the washing machine. "Do I look like the Maytag man?" he said.

The third night he came home, and his wife said, "Well, everything's fixed."

"Who fixed them?" her husband asked.

"The mailman did it."

"What did you have to pay him?"

"Well, I had the choice of baking him a cake or going to bed with him."

"What flavor of cake did you bake him?"

"Do I look like Betty Crocker?" she said.

Judge Ralph McClanahan

IRVINE, KENTUCKY

Some Accomplishment

When Tex Rickard, Jack London, Rex Beach, and Robert Service were in the Alaska Gold Rush of 1897, Wilson Mizner was also a pal of theirs. They were about as tough a bunch as you could find.

One day Wilson Mizner and Tex Rickard were standing and talking when Rickard pulled a gun and shot a man through his sombrero.

"What's the idea?" asked Mizner.

"You know my gal Goldie?" asked the excited Tex. "Well, that rat insulted her!"

"For God's sake," said Mizner, *"how?"*

Ed Ward

BLEDSOE, KENTUCKY

No Kin

This fellow whose name was Bob Earl was settin' back on the porch of his cabin, and he was kind of sad. His mama, who was sweeping up the house, said "Bob Earl, what's the matter with you?"

He said, "Well, Ma, I'm gettin' to that age where I'm goin' to go find me a girlfriend. I told Daddy that I want to take out Janie Lee. He told me I musn't do that 'cause she's kind of like a cousin of mine. And so then I told him that Sara Lou would do and I'd go ask Sara Lou to go out walking with me, but Daddy told me I shouldn't do that 'cause she's kind of kin to me. So then I said Ellie June is the only other good-looking girl in the whole county, I reckon I'd better take her, but he says she's a cousin of mine, too. I don't know what to do, 'cause there just isn't anyone else I want to take out."

His mama went on sweeping for a minute, and finally she said, "Bob Earl, don't you pay no attention to your daddy. He ain't no kin to you."

Katie Letcher Lyle

LEXINGTON, VIRGINIA

Available, But...

Little girl to lady teacher: "Are you married? If you're not, my daddy has been divorced three times."

Susan Jones
SWANNANOA, NORTH CAROLINA

Too Much Learning...

A man and his wife were out raking leaves. After a while, his wife went over and kicked him.

"What was that for?" he asked.

"For being such a lousy lover," she said.

He raked on for a while, and then went over and kicked her.

"What was that for?" she asked.

"For knowing the difference," he said.

George Lindsey
NASHVILLE, TENNESSEE

Making Plans

An older man and woman were sitting on the front porch of their mountain home looking out across the valley, rocking away in their rocking chairs. After about fifteen minutes of silence, the husband said, "Sarah, I've been thinking. If one of us should die, I believe I'll move to California."

Judge Ray Corns
FRANKFORT, KENTUCKY

If I Was to Die...

This couple sat down on a sofa near me at a convention where I was speaking. The man said to his wife, "Helen, if I was to die, would you get married again?"

She said, "I don't know. I've never thought about it."

He said, "Well, if you *did* get married again, would you let him live in my house?"

She said, "I don't know. I've not thought about that either, but if he didn't have one..."

He went on, "Would you let him drive my car?"

She said, "Well, if he didn't have one, I might…"
He rushed on, "Would you let him use my golf clubs?"
She said, "No, he's left-handed."

Joe Bly
ASHEVILLE, NORTH CAROLINA

Upset

A man suspected his wife of infidelity. This bothered him, and he talked about it a lot with his fellow workers. One morning he came in and said, "I was right. I went home early from work yesterday and caught her with another man."

"What did you do?" asked one of his co-workers.

"It made me so mad I didn't eat nary a bite of supper and very little for breakfast."

Charles Morgan
BEREA, KENTUCKY

In the Family

A woman whose husband often came home drunk decided to cure him of the habit. One Hallowe'en night, she put on a devil suit and hid behind a tree to intercept him on the way home.

When her husband came by, she jumped out and stood before him with her red horns, long tail, and pitchfork.

"Who are you?" he asked.

"I'm the Devil," she responded.

"Well, come on home with me," he said, "I married your sister."

Rev. E. Ray Jones
CLEARWATER, FLORIDA

Suggestion

Husband: "Every morning when I shave, I feel fifteen years younger."

Wife: "Why don't you shave at night?"

Lester Cope
BEAN STATION, TENNESSEE

He's Handy

A man went into a barber shop to get a shave, and since the manicurist was really beautiful, he asked for a manicure at the same time. He kept looking at her, really taken with her, and finally said, "How about going out with me tonight?"

She said, "No, I'm married."

He said, "Well, just tell your husband you're busy tonight."

"Tell him yourself," she said. "He's shaving you."

Bill Hastings
BEREA, KENTUCKY

Transformation

Husband: "I know a woman who lived to the age of forty without learning to read or write. Then she met a man who made a scholar out of her in two years."

Wife: "That's nothing. I know a man who was a scholar at forty, but he met a woman who made a fool out of him in thirty minutes."

James E. Atz
MILTOWN, INDIANA

No Forecaster

A husband and wife were in bed sound asleep one night, and the phone rang. The husband answered it and then said, "How in the hell should I know. It's four hundred fifty miles from here!" and slammed the phone down.

His wife asked, "What was that about?"

He said, "I don't know. Some man wanted to know if the coast is clear."

Bob Spera
CLINTWOOD, VIRGINIA

Yours Or Mine?

Two yuppies got married and pitched right in working as hard as they could to get ahead. After about ten years, they were prospering—big house in the suburbs, two BMWs, good bank account and stock portfolio, contributing a hundred dollars a year to the Republican Party—but they were tired of hustling so hard.

One night they were in their suburban home by the fire doing homework, and there was a little old lady sitting there in a rocking chair, knitting.

The wife said, "Why don't we take a long vacation, maybe go on a cruise or something. We've earned it."

"That sounds good," her husband said, "but what about your mother?"

"My mother!" she said. "I thought she was your mother!"

Jim Adams
MIDDLESBORO, KENTUCKY

Fitting the Need

Two women got to talking at the supermarket, and one asked the other, "How many times have you been married?"

"Four times, " she answered.

"What were their professions?" the other one asked.

"A millionaire, an actor, a preacher and an undertaker—one for the money, two for the show, three to get ready and four to go."

Glenn "Buddy" Westbrook
LONDON, KENTUCKY

Through Thick and Thin

This fellow had a bad car accident, and he woke up in the hospital, and his wife Ethel, with just a few scratches, was sitting by his side.

He got his bearings and then said, "Ethel, do you remember when I broke my leg when we were hiking? You were right there with me. Do you remember when I got kicked by that mule, and you were right there with me? Do you remember that time that tree fell and knocked me down, and you were right there with me? And now we had this car wreck, and you were right there with me. Ethel," he said. "You're bad luck!"

John Holbrook
MOUNT VERNON, KENTUCKY

Even Better

A woman went to her preacher and said she and her husband were having trouble, he was mean to her, and she was going to sue for divorce.

The preacher said, "The Bible says to be kind to those who revile you and thereby heap coals of fire on their heads." Then he asked, "Have you tried heaping coals of fire on his head?"

"No," she said, "but I've thrown scalding water on him a few times."

Shirley Jones
MARBLE, NORTH CAROLINA

Fairy Tale

Once, a small girl and her mother were talking. The little girl said, "Mommy, do fairy tales always begin with 'Once upon a time'?"

"No," replied her mother. "Some begin with, 'Honey, I have to work late tonight.'"

Willie Aaron
ALBANY, KENTUCKY

For Whom the Bell Tolls

My story comes from an earlier time when life was lived at a slower pace. It was told to me many years ago by a physician friend when I first began my practice. He told this story as a true one on himself. I think its humor is ageless.

George had a bright future. He was home for the summer after his second year of medical school and was dating Effie Miller, the daughter of Henry Miller, a moderately well-to-do farmer, landholder, and respected member of the community.

The Miller family all lived together in a big, two-story, white frame farm house, the kind with gingerbread trim on the eaves and a big porch around three sides. Now, these porches were the family's summertime center for relaxation, recreation, and socializing. It was George's routine to call on Effie every Sunday morning. He would then go to church with the family, and after church he would come home and eat dinner with them. After dinner, he and Effie would sit on the swing on the spacious back porch.

Now, on this particular Sunday afternoon, some dozen or more close friends, neighbors, and relatives of the family had gathered on the porch. The women were on one end and the men were on the other. Effie and George occupied the swing in the middle. Two of the younger children were playing hide-and-go-seek around the house and out-buildings, and two of the older children, Effie's younger brothers, were cranking up the ice-cream freezer. Later on that afternoon, everyone would be served a dish of ice cream made from fresh strawberries and cream so thick you had to dip it out with a jar.

It was a beautiful early summer day. A rain the previous night made everything look fresh, clean, and bright. A gentle breeze blew the length of the porch and stirred the tresses of the giant elm tree at its end and brought the sweet smell of wild honeysuckle to George's nose. A mockingbird perched in the top of a nearby pear tree sang its heart out, and hollyhocks were in full bloom against the back picket fence. But most satisfying of all to George, he had his arm around a beautiful girl, his future wife. He had never been in higher spirits or felt better.

Then, without warning, his tranquility was abruptly shattered by a low-grade cramp in his lower abdomen. He thought, "It must be those sweet potatoes I ate for dinner." He tried to ignore his discomfort, but the gas bubble kept growing, and so did George's discomfort. He searched his mind for a solution to his problem. He thought of excusing himself to go get a drink of water, but a pitcher of ice water sat on a nearby table. And he couldn't just get up and leave unobtrusively, sitting as he did between the women on one end of the porch and the men on the other end. So he sat there and suffered.

As he sat in his discomfort, George happened to look off to the left and saw a rope hanging down past the eave of the house. He knew this rope was attached to a big dinner bell atop a post just off the porch. A light went on in his head. He had the solution to his problem! He had no time to spare, so he put his plan into action. He accidently (on purpose) knocked his hat off toward the dangling rope, got up as if to retrieve his hat, took two or three steps in the direction of the rope, and faked a stumble. As he fell, he reached out as if to break his fall but instead grabbed the rope and gave it a hearty pull.

Now, just the other day, one of the kids he knew had run along the porch and given the rope a yank, and the loud BONG-BONG of the bell was deafening. So George gave the rope a yank. At the same time he pulled on the rope, the gas bubble was released. No one would be the wiser, he thought, because you could literally hear that bell for a country mile.

Alas, alas!

The loud noise heard from one end of the porch to the other was *not* the bell. It would not toll for George today. Someone had removed the clapper!

Dr. Bill Epling
SUN CITY CENTER, FLORIDA

A Second Honeymoon

Al Boyles of Raleigh, North Carolina, who proposed to his wife, Mary Eva, after knowing her for only two weeks decided to celebrate forty-three years of married life by taking her on a second honeymoon.

After a long and tiring all-day drive to get to the Netherlands Plaza Hotel in Cincinnati, they decided a nice warm bubble bath would be welcome, so Al went to the bathroom and turned on the water. While he was waiting for the tub to

40

fill, he popped the cork on a bottle of champagne, poured them each a glass, and they sat relaxing in the living room of their hotel suite. They were having such a nice time sipping champagne and talking, Al forgot about the bath water altogether.

Ten or fifteen minutes later, there was a banging on his door, and when he opened it, he received the brunt of some pretty bad language. "Now, wait just a minute," he told the angry man, "watch your language. I've got a lady in the room here with me."

"Well, what do you think I've got in mine," the red-faced gent came back, "a duck?!"

The Birthday Present

One year Mary Eva told Al, "Honey, I've bought you an unusual birthday present."

"What did you buy me?" he asked her.

"A cemetery plot."

He accepted it and agreed with her that it was unusual. The next year, she didn't buy him a gift, so he asked her why.

"Because," she said, "you didn't use the one I bought you last year!"

Al Boyles
RALEIGH, NORTH CAROLINA

Phonus Interruptus

My wife and I have been married thirty-four years. We were romantically inclined this morning, but right in the middle of our adventure the phone rang. My wife said, "You get it, I've still got two more nails to polish."

It was my son calling long distance. He said, "Dad, I've got a problem here. I let the little dog out this morning, and the dog across the street came right over and locked onto her. I don't know what to do. I've tried just about everything—the hose, the broom. Do you have any ideas?"

"Yes, I do have a suggestion," I told him. "Why don't you take the longest phone extension you have and put the

41

phone on the porch. You hang up, I'll hang up. And then maybe the ringing of the phone when I call you back will break them up."

He said, "Okay, I'll try that. But do you think it'll work?"

I said, "Well, it worked on your mother and me."

Brian McFarland

ONTARIO, CANADA

"A Closed Mouth Gathers No Feet"

P R O V E R B S   A N D   E P I G R A M S

Time is Nature's way of making sure that everything doesn't happen all at once.

Albert Stewart
HINDMAN, KENTUCKY

The following sayings were collected by Dilly Wilson, of Berea, Kentucky.

Q: Why did the chicken cross the road?
A: To show the 'possum it can be done.

Money doesn't bring you happiness, but it enables you to look for it in more places.

Your conscience may not keep you from doing wrong, but it sure keeps you from enjoying it.

Middle age is when broadness of the mind and narrowness of the waist change places.

Honesty is the best policy, but not always the best politics.

When you're getting kicked from behind, that means you're in front.

Misers aren't much fun to live with, but they make great ancestors.

Be careful what rut you choose. You may be in it the rest of your life.

The trouble with bucket seats is that not everybody has the same size bucket.

When you see the handwriting on the wall, you can bet you're in a public building.

Opportunities always look bigger going than coming.

The real reason you can't take it with you is that it goes before you do.

Advertisement: "Let me do your income tax. I'll save you time (about 20 years)."

Never get in a fuss with those who buy ink by the barrel.

Junk is something you throw away three weeks before you need it.

Drive as you wish your kids would.

Hospitality is making your guests feel at home, even if you wish they were.

A closed mouth gathers no feet.

A man who can smile when things go wrong has found someone to blame it on.

Talk is cheap because supply exceeds demand.

A modern pioneer is a woman who can get through a rainy Saturday with a television on the blink.

Nothing is harder on your laurels than resting on them.

Minor operations are those performed on other people.

The world is full of willing people: some willing to work and some willing to let them.

Light travels faster than sound. That's why some folks appear bright until they speak.

If you want to be sure you never forget your wife's birthday, just try forgetting it once.

I was pleasantly surprised to hear that on a written test eighty percent of football players made straight A's. They didn't do too bad on the rest of the alphabet either.

To find a girl's faults, praise her to her girlfriends.

Money isn't everything—there's credit cards, money orders, and travelers checks.

Some people are like blisters. They don't show up until the work is done.

He who falls in love with himself will have no rivals.

Nothing is more expensive than a girl who's free for the evening.

She may be good for nothing but is never bad for nothing.

She doesn't care for a man's company unless he owns it.

In telling fish tales, the first liar doesn't have a chance.

Regarding age, I have too much sand in the bottom of my hourglass.

A true friend is one that lets his grass grow as tall as his neighbor's.

Ever notice...
>...that no matter where you sit at a ballgame, you're always between the hot dog peddler and his best customer?
>...that a dog's affection increases in direct proportion with how wet he is?
>...that no matter how crowded a room is, there's always room for one bore.
>...that the waitress always comes around to ask how your food is when you have your mouth full?

Here are a few from Judge Ray Corns of Frankfort, Kentucky:

Poverty is a condition we try to conceal at the time but brag about in our memoirs.

A babysitter is a teenager acting like an adult while the adults are out acting like teenagers.

It's better to marry for money than for no reason at all.

Many of the happiest hours of my life were spent in the arms of another man's wife—my mother's.

Going to church doesn't make you a Christian any more than going to a garage makes you a mechanic.

If you don't know where you're going, you're never lost.

And a few from another great Kentucky humorist, John Ed McConnell of Louisville:

I ate at a restaurant that was so bad the cook wouldn't even lick his fingers.

To do good is noble. To tell others to do good is also noble and a lot less trouble.

Conscience is the weak inner voice that sometimes doesn't speak your language.

Confidence is the feeling you have before you really understand the problem.

Experience is a wonderful thing. It enables you to recognize a mistake when you make it again.

"Glad to Go to Bed with Ben Gay..."

A G I N G

Compensation

There are four advantages to getting old and forgetful: One, you meet new friends every day; two, every joke you hear is new; three, you can hide your own Easter eggs; and I forget the fourth thing.

Buddy Westbrook
LONDON, KENTUCKY

Longevity

This fellow who was about seventy-six went to the doctor for the first time in his life, and so the doctor had to take his history.

The doctor said, "I need to ask some of these questions so I can find out what's wrong with you and treat you. What did your father die of?"

He said, "My father? Why, Pappy ain't dead. He *is* bed-rid..."

And the doctor said, "I'm sure he is. If you're seventy-six, then he must be pretty feeble."

The fellow said, "Well, not usually, but he got into a fight with Granddaddy."

The doctor was flabbergasted. Said, "He got into a fight with your grandfather? My goodness. What over?"

The fellow said, "Well, actually, it was over a woman, but it's OK. Granddaddy married her and Daddy's kind of blue."

The doctor couldn't believe this, and he said, "Why in the world would a man the age of your grandfather want to get married?"

The man said, "Well, nobody said he *wanted* to."

Katie Letcher Lyle

LEXINGTON, VIRGINIA

Old Folks are Worth a Fortune

Silver in their hair,
Gold in their teeth,
Stones in their kidneys,
Lead in their feet and
Gas in their stomachs.

Lewis Lamb

PAINT LICK, KENTUCKY

The Gentlemen Callers

I have become a little older since I saw you last, and a few changes have come to my life since then. Frankly, I have become quite a frivolous ole gal. I am seeing five gentlemen daily. As soon as I wake up, Will Power helps me get out of bed. Then I go see John. Then Charlie Horse comes along, and when he is here, he takes a lot of time and attention. When he leaves, Arthur Ritis shows up and stays the rest of the day. He doesn't like to stay in one place very long, so he takes me from joint to joint. After such a busy day, I'm really tired and glad to go to bed with Ben Gay.

Lewis Lamb

PAINT LICK, KENTUCKY

Thinking on the Hereafter

The Preacher came to call the other day. He said at my age, I should be thinking about the hereafter. I told him, "Oh, I do all the time. No matter where I am—in the parlor, upstairs, in the kitchen, or down in the basement, I ask myself, 'Now, what am I here after?'"

Lewis Lamb

PAINT LICK, KENTUCKY

A Bit Vague

Three old men were talking one day about how they forget things.

The first one said, "Sometimes I get undressed to get into the shower, and suddenly I can't remember whether I'm getting into the shower or getting out."

The second one said, "Well, sometimes I find myself on the stairs, and I can't remember whether I'm going up or coming down."

The third one said, "Well, so far I haven't had that trouble. I'll just knock on wood and hope it doesn't happen to me."

He did, and then he said, "I wonder who that is?"

Pat Wagner

MOORES CREEK, KENTUCKY

Registered and Certified

One time, this friend of mine said, "I'd like to go over into Tennessee and look for some antiques." She collected them. So I said I'd go with her. We drove over the mountain and were looking in different antique shops, when at one place, she called me over to the counter and said, "Look here. Here's one of those brass buckles you've been wanting." I looked at it but said, "No, that's just one of these contemporary reproductions. I want a real old, old, authentic brass belt buckle."

Well, months later comes in the mail at Christmas time this present she had got for me. It was in a white canvas bank bag, and it said on the front of the bag, "Wells Fargo Bank, San Francisco, California." I opened up the bag, and there was this buckle—I bet it weighed a pound and a half—had a Wells Fargo stagecoach on the front of it. I looked on the back, and there was this long serial number, and there was a card inside the bag that said, "If you will sign this card and drop it in the mail, we will register your name and your belt buckle in the Wells Fargo Bank vault in San Francisco." I said to myself, "Now *there's* an authentic belt buckle."

Well, you know how it is when you get something for Christmas, you want to show it off. I was going to visit my brother in Winston-Salem. My daddy was visiting my brother there at Christmas. I stopped at a place in Hickory— it's about half-way—to get a sandwich and a cup of coffee. When I went up to pay my check, there was this twenty-year-old woman at the cash register.

As I walked up, I reared back to show off my buckle, reached her my money and check, and said, "It's registered in the Wells Fargo Bank in San Francisco."

She said, "Old man, you'd better get out of here or I'll call my father and he'll knock you out in the middle of the road!"

Well, I went out to the parking lot wondering what her problem was, and looked down, and my pants were unzipped.

I got to Winston-Salem and was telling Daddy about it. Said, "Well, Daddy, I need your advice. I'm afraid I'm getting senile. I forgot to zip up."

He said, "No, son, senile is when you forget to zip down."

Joe Bly
ASHEVILLE, NORTH CAROLINA

Total Strangers

There was a woman who loved the Elderhostel program, which offers classes all over the country for older people. She signed up for a particular course at a small college, but when she arrived, she was told by the director that they were full and could not take anyone else. She protested.

"But you must take me. I've waited for so long to take this course by Professor So-and-So. Please, isn't there some way?"

She was told the problem was that there were not enough rooms at the local hotel to hold everybody. Then the director had a thought. "There is one single gentleman in a double room. If you could work out something with him, you could register."

So she went to see this man. Knocked on his door. He opened it, and she explained her problem and asked if she could stay with him. Said, "I'll be glad to sleep on that couch. I won't be any problem."

He said, "Look. I don't know you. You don't know me. We don't know any of those other people, and they don't know us, so I don't see why not."

She registered for the program, and she and the gentleman retired to their room after the first session. He went to the bathroom, changed into his pajamas, and went to bed. She went to the bathroom, got changed into her nightgown, and lay down on the couch. After a while, she started tossing around. Couldn't get to sleep. Finally, she said, "This couch is so lumpy and hard, I just can't get comfortable. Do you think it would be all right if I just lay on top of the covers on the other side of your bed?"

He said, "Look, I don't know you. You don't know me. We don't know any of those other people, and they don't know us. So why not?"

So she got up on top of the bed with him. She lay there for quite a while, and then she said, "I'm cold. I just can't sleep. Do you think it would be all right if I just got under the covers. I'll stay on my side of the bed?"

He said, " Look I don't know you. You don't know me. We don't know any of those other people, and they don't know us. I don't see why not."

So she got down under the covers. She lay there for a while, and then she said, "Would you like to have a party?"

He said, "Look, I don't know you. You don't know me. We don't know any of those other people, and they don't know us. Who would we invite?"

Versions from Hilda Woodie
and Bill French, both of
BEREA, KENTUCKY

"I'd Hate to Feel This Bad and Then Find Out I'm Well"

HEALTH

Reverent

Dr. Paul Spray is a fine orthopedic surgeon at the Oak Ridge, Tennessee, Hospital, and he is frequently paged over the public address system.

One day after he had been paged several times, a woman said, "Boy, this sure is a religious hospital."

I asked, "Why do you say that?"

"Because they pause every so often and say, 'Doctors pray.'"

> *Charles Kirby*
> OAK RIDGE, TENNESSEE

Tough

We have some tough people up here in West Virginia.

This guy got sick and went to see a doctor, and he had to have an appendectomy. The doctor put him in the hospital and operated on him right away. The next day, this guy got up, put on his clothes, and was walking out of the hospital when he ran into the doctor, who said, "Hey fellow, you're going to have to get back in bed, or you'll bust your stitches out."

The patient said, "What do you mean? Did you use cheap thread or what?"

Paul Lepp
SOUTH CHARLESTON, WEST VIRGINIA

Feeling Bad

A fellow went to see the doctor, and while he was being examined, he said, "Boy, I sure hope I'm sick."

The doctor said, "That's a bad attitude you've got."

The fellow said, "Well, I'd sure hate to feel this bad and then find out I'm well."

Loyal Jones

Chances Are...

According to statistics, one out of four people in the United States is unbalanced. There's no need to be too concerned unless you have three friends who seem perfectly normal.

Scott McIntosh
FLOSSMOOR, ILLINOIS

Positive Proof

A man was bad to drink, and the temperance workers got after him from time to time, to little avail. Finally, they came up with a plan they thought was foolproof. They went to see him with a bottle of liquor and a live worm. They poured whiskey into a glass and then dropped in the worm— which immediately expired and sank to the bottom of the glass.

"What does that show you?" they asked.

After studying the situation a minute, the man said, "If you drink liquor, you'll never have worms."

Dorothy Wierwille
CINCINNATI, OHIO

56

Depends

A woman took her elderly father to a clinic for an examination, and when they went by the clinic pharmacy, she inquired, "Do you need to get any medicine, Daddy?"

"Well, I don't know,"he said. "What have they got?"

Loyal Jones

Kentucky Medical Terminology for the Layman

Artery: The study of fine paintings
Barium: What to do when C.P.R. fails
Benign: What you be after you be eight
Caesarean section: A district in Rome
Colic: A sheep dog
Congenital: Friendly
Dilate: Live long
Fester: Quicker
GI series: Baseball games between teams of soldiers
Hangnail: A coat hook
Medical staff: A doctor's cane
Minor operation: Coal digging
Morbid: A higher offer
Nitrate: Lower than the day rate
Node: Was aware of
Organic: Church musician
Outpatient: A person who has fainted
Postoperative: A letter carrier
Protein: In favor of young people
Secretion: Hiding anything
Serology: A study of English knighthood
Tablet: A small table
Tumor: An extra pair
Urine: Opposite of "you're out"
Varicose veins: Veins very close together

Junior Deaton

AGES, KENTUCKY

A Real Smoker

A fellow goes to the doctor on behalf of his grandmother back a long time ago and says, "We're worried about Granny's smoking. We know she's ninety and all, but we want her to last a long time. She just smokes all the time."

The doctor says, "Well, she's lived this long. I wouldn't worry about it."

The fellow says, "Yeah, but she inhales."

The doctor says, "Well, lots of people do."

The fellow says, "Yeah, but Granny, she don't exhale."

Katie Letcher Lyle
LEXINGTON, VIRGINIA

A Miracle

A man had arthritis in his hands and went for orthopedic surgery. He woke up with bandages on both hands. When the surgeon came in, he asked, "Doc, will I be able to play the the piano when I get the bandages off?"

The doctor said, "I don't see why not."

"That's just great, Doc," he said. "I've never been able to before."

Loyal Jones

Either Way

An expectant mother was being rushed to the hospital but didn't quite make it. She gave birth to her baby on the hospital lawn. Later, the father received a bill, listing "Delivery Room Fee: $500."

He wrote the hospital and reminded them that the baby was born on the front lawn. A week passed, and a corrected bill arrived: "Greens Fee: $200."

Marje Gowins
FRANKFORT, KENTUCKY

It Only Hurts When I Laugh

It hasn't been a very good year for me. I was playing golf this spring and got hit with a golf ball right in the side of the face. I suffered a broken jaw and had to get it wired up, and it was very uncomfortable.

I went back to the golf club a couple of weeks later and ran into the manager. He quickly invited me in and commiserated with my injury. He said, "Can I get you something to eat?"

I mumbled, "No, the doctor says I'm not supposed to eat solid foods with my jaw wired up like this."

He said, "How about something to drink?"

"No, the doctor says I can't drink anything since I'm on antibiotics."

"Oh, I understand," he said. "You know that guy that hit you with that golf ball was so upset, he came into the bar, downed sixteen drinks, went out and jumped into his car, and drove eighty miles an hour down the road right into a tree and was killed instantly."

I said, "That's another thing the doctor told me. I'm not supposed to laugh!"

Brian McFarland
ONTARIO, CANADA

"Don't Let This Land Fool You"

FARMS AND FARMERS

Gentle Revenge

I used to help out a Quaker farmer in the mornings because he was milking about twenty-three cows. One morning it was really bad cold outside. It was so cold everything outside was froze as stiff as a woodpecker's lip. Really bad! We slipped and slid getting down there to the barn, about an inch of ice and downhill—slick as deer guts on a doorknob.

He started milking one of the cows, and the cow swished her tail around a couple of times and knocked the bucket of milk over. Very patiently, didn't say anything, he just picked that bucket back up and sat back down on his little two-legged stool, and about when he got the bucket half full, she hit that thing with her foot and turned it over again. I was watching him then, to see if he was going to do anything, but he didn't. He sort of gritted his teeth and started milking again. He got it about a third full, and she kicked that bucket again, knocked it over, and knocked him over backwards.

He got up and said, "Bossy, I will not strike thee. I will hold my temper and not do harm unto thee. But if thou kick the pail again, I will sell thee to a Baptist, and he'll beat the hell out of thee!"

Dr. Bill Foster
FLORENCE, ALABAMA

Sort of...

Two men met for the first time since they were boys together. One wanted to find out about the other one and his brothers.

"What is Dick doing?"

"Well, he's sort of an artist."

"And what about Bill?"

"Well, he's sort of a writer."

"And Tom?"

"He's sort of a preacher."

"And what about you. What are you doing?"

"Well, I'm sort of a farmer—and feeding Dick, Bill and Tom."

Loyal Jones

Rock Farm

I was out in the country one day watching an old fellow plowing on a hillside. It was a real rock farm, and I'd never seen anything that looked as bad as it did. I was fascinated watching him trying to farm that field.

I waited until he got back around on his tractor and stopped nearby. As he pulled out his handkerchief and wiped his brow, I said, "Mister, I've seen some farm land, but I've never seen anything quite like this."

He said, "Son, don't let this land fool you. It's a whole lot sorrier than it looks!"

Bob Hannah
ATLANTA, GEORGIA

Some Collision

These city people were driving down this country road when a farmer ran out and flagged them down, shouting, "I need your help and ain't got time to explain."

He led them to a cow who was straining to give birth to a calf, but it was a breech birth and she was having a hard time. The calf's rear feet were sticking out of the cow, and the farmer directed them to grab hold and tug as hard as they could. Directly, they delivered the calf, and the farmer thanked them warmly.

Then one of the city fellows said, "There's just one thing I want to ask. Just how fast was that little one going when it hit the big one?"

Janice Steirn
HUNTINGTON, WEST VIRGINIA

Old Maude

I was raised in Garrard County, Kentucky, on a rough farm. We had to work hard for a living, me and Daddy, and one evening we were chopping corn, and Daddy said, "Now, we want to get done today if we can." But it got late in the evening, and Daddy finally said, "Well, we ain't a-goin' to get done, so let's just quit."

We come to the house, took our baths, and set down to supper. There was a big Holiness meeting going on up the road there, so Daddy said, "I'll tell ye, son, we'll go up there tonight."

I said, "Well, that suits me all right."

We had an old mare that mother driv, and we called her Maude—old faithful Maude. She near-about raised us children. We hooked her to the buggy and started up the road to church. We got pretty near the church, and old Maude quit. Well, Daddy coaxed her every way in the world trying to get her to go, but finally he flew mad and grabbed a whip and went to beating her, but all he did was to break his whip. Well, he was one of these fellers that wouldn't give up. He'd stay until the last cat was hung!

63

He said, "We're going to church." So he built a fire under old Maude, but all she done was was move up a little piece and and burned the buggy up!

Daddy said, "We'll go anyhow. We'll ride her!" We took her loose from the shaves and done her harness up, and me and Daddy got up on her. We almost got to the church house when she quit again. Daddy said, "Well, what are we a-goin' to do now?"

I said, "You lead her, and I'll get a brush and get behind her and hit her—make her go."

So I gave her a whump, and she jumped right a-straddle of Daddy! Well, he kind of scolded me a little, but went on, tied old Maude up behind the church to a post.

It was getting pretty late by this time, and Daddy was tired out and all, but we went in and sat down. The service was going good by that time, but all at once, Daddy fell over asleep—wore-out, you know. Then he got to snoring, and people started watching and listening to Daddy instead of the preacher. He lay there and snored for while, so the preacher finally just closed up his Bible and quit. He gave the invitation, and a big woman weighed about three hundred pounds came prancing down the aisle, lost her balance, and fell right a-straddle of Daddy!

Now, Daddy was laying there dreaming about old Maude, so when that woman set down on him, he yelled, "Jake, cut her belly band! Take off her bridle and turn her loose and let her go! She's a-riding me without a saddle!"

Jake Lamb
PAINT LICK, KENTUCKY

Bad Mule

This fellow down in Georgia had a real mean mule which had kicked him and broken both of his legs, so he put him up for sale.

A young man came up there. Said, "I'd like to buy your mule. How much do you want for him?"

The fellow said, "I'm not going to tell you how much I want for him. First of all, where do you live?"

The young man said, "What difference does it make where I live?"

"It makes a lot of difference," he said. "Where do you live?"

So, he said, "I live over in Dahlonega."

"That's not far enough."

"What d'you mean 'that's not far enough'?"

The owner said, "I'm not going to sell this mule to anybody who lives within two hundred miles of here. Not only do I not want to see this mule again, I don't want to hear any conversations about him!"

Bob Hannah
ATLANTA, GEORGIA

Another Bad Mule

This boy was out plowing a mule that was bad to kick, and a neighbor came along and said, "Son, I know that mule is bad to kick. Has he ever kicked you?"

"No, sir," he said, "but several times he's kicked right where I've been."

Bob Hannah
ATLANTA, GEORGIA

Staying Even

The county extension agent went out to see an old farmer he hadn't yet visited.

"How are you doing?" he asked.

"I guess I'm holding my own," the farmer said. "I didn't have anything when I started farming, and I ain't got anything yet."

Loyal Jones

Caught On Fast

While milking a cow on a hot, humid, August evening, a farmer was aggravated by the cow's tail hitting him in the face. He finally tied the cow's tail to his right leg.

"Before I had been around the barn seven times," the farmer said, "I knew I had made a mistake."

Judge Ray Corns
FRANKFORT, KENTUCKY

Knows Enough Already

A county extension agent went out to visit with a farmer who wasn't exactly prospering. After looking over his operation, he invited him to attend a short course he had set up on scientific farming.

The farmer reflected for a minute and then said, "No, I don't believe I'll come. I don't farm nearly as good as I know how to now."

Loyal Jones

Dad Wouldn't Do

I come from a large family; there were sixteen of us kids. I thought my name was Git-Some-Wood until I was twelve years old.

My brother was Git-Some-More-Wood.

I was late to school one day, and I told my teacher that I was late because I had to take the cow to the bull to be serviced. She said, "Couldn't your father have done it?"

I said, "No, teacher, it had to be the bull!"

Brian McFarland
ONTARIO, CANADA

Stud Fee

There was a farmer who had a prize bull he used for breeding purposes. One day he had to take his wife to the dentist. He left his daughter at home and told her, "Honey, we're neighborly and friendly around here, so if anyone comes to use the bull, just tell them to help themselves. The fee is five dollars."

She said, "I can handle that."

They'd hardly got out of sight when a man walked up and asked to see her father. She told him her parents were gone, but if it was about the bull, she could handle it. He said, "No, I have to see your daddy."

A couple of hours passed, and the man came back again, asked, "Has your daddy come back yet?"

She said, "No, but if it's about the bull, I can handle it."

He said, "No, I've got to see your daddy." He looked like he was getting a little red-faced and mad.

The third time he came back and found her parents still gone, he said to the girl, "Well, I'll just tell you what it is. Your brother had been taking my daughter out, and now she's in the family way. I've got to ask your daddy what he's going to do about it."

She said, "Well, it's five dollars for the *bull*, but I don't know what he gets for my brother."

Billy Edd Wheeler

Time To Sell

My Grandpa was sort of a self-taught veterinarian. We were in Claude Stewart's store one day when someone came up and said, "Garland..." (That was my Grandpa's name. He had a sister named Rose, a sister named Lily, a sister named Iris; so when he was born, they named him Garland.) "Garland, I got a problem. My mule limps one day and the next day he don't. I've tried everything, but I can't figure it out. What should I do?"

Grandpa said, "The next day that he don't limp, *sell* him!"

Dr. Bill Foster
FLORENCE, ALABAMA

"It's the Principal of the Thing..."

SCHOOLS AND EDUCATION

A Catch to It

I always liked school. It was the principal of the thing I hated.

Paul Kusco
WISE, VIRGINIA

Passing it On

We had a character in our town who didn't finish the third grade, but he had a son who graduated from the university and made straight A's the whole four years. He was one of the few who had ever done it.

Someone said to the father, "How did he do it?"

"It was simple," he said. "I just taught him all I knowed, and then he picked up a little bit along the way."

Charles Tribble
CYNTHIANA, KENTUCKY

Leave it Alone

First professor: "Do you know how to cure a dean?"
Second professor: "No."
First professor: "Good."

Dr. Jim W. Miller
BOWLING GREEN, KENTUCKY

Wish and De-Wish

There were three guys marooned on an island, two preachers and a college president. After they were marooned there for several weeks, a bottle floated up, and one of them went and got it.

Said, "Do you reckon there could be…."

One of the others said, "Well, there might be…."

One of them pulled the cork out of that bottle, rubbed it, and a genie came out and said, "Each one of you can have one wish, so what do you want?"

One of the ministers said, "You know, I miss my congregation so much, I wish I was back there with them." He was gone!

The other preacher said, "I miss my wife and family so much, I wish I was back there with them." Poof, he was gone too.

The genie looked at the college president and said, "You have a wish as well. What do you want?"

He thought a minute and said, "You know, I'm just not used to making a decision on my own. I wish those other two fellows were back here."

John Stephenson
PRESIDENT, BEREA COLLEGE

Matter of Perspective

When my father was a high school principal, a single woman teacher came to him and asked him if he would write a letter to the mother of one of her students. The boy helped his father work on the farm and the odor from his unwashed body, mixed with smells from the barn, was pretty strong.

The teacher said she had to keep a window open, even in the winter.

So, my father wrote the letter and received this reply:

"My son don't stink. He smells just like his father. The problem is with yer damned old maid teacher. She don't know how a good man smells."

Jim Hinsdale
WARSAW, KENTUCKY

Those Prepositions

A country fellow ends up on the campus of Vanderbilt University. "Where's the library at?" he asks somebody passing by. He says, "Here at Vanderbilt, we don't end sentences with prepositions."

The country fellow scratches his head a minute and says, "OK, where's the library at, jackass?"

Katie Letcher Lyle
LEXINGTON, VIRGINIA

Whatever Pleases You

A country school board had a teacher prospect in to size him up. One member asked him whether the earth was round or flat. He didn't bat an eye. "I don't know how you people feel about it, but I can teach it either way."

The late Dr. Eslie Asbury
CARLISLE, KENTUCKY

Not Mine

A teacher was having trouble teaching arithmetic to one little boy. So she said, "If you reached in your right pocket and found a nickel, and you reached in your left pocket and found another one, what would you have?"

"Somebody else's pants," said the little boy.

Loyal Jones

How Can That Help?

A third grade teacher told her class on the first day of school, "If any of you need to go to the bathroom, just hold up two fingers."

A little boy on the back row said, "I don't see how that's going to help a bit."

Judge Ray Corns
FRANKFORT, KENTUCKY

Wet Spots in the Garden

I used to teach kindergarten for the Christian Appalachian Project down by the Appalachian Village near Berea. One day I sent the boys into the bathroom to get washed up for lunch, and just a minute later, Brian came running back out and said, "Teacher, Frankie peed on me, on my new pants!"

Well, I waited for the offending party to come out. When he did I said "Frankie, Brian is a little upset. He says that you peed on his pants."

He didn't say a word, just looked down.

"Frankie, now there's a big wet spot on Brian's new pants."

Frankie exploded and said, "Well, how was I supposed to know they were new?!"

Lisa Raymer
BEREA, KENTUCKY

Too Much Education

A North Carolina school committeeman informed his neighbor that the school board had decided not to renew for an additional year the contract of the man who taught science at the high school. The neighbor expressed his surprise at the action of the board, saying he understood that this particular teacher had attended many colleges and earned many degrees.

The school committeeman replied, "That's the trouble with him. He has been educated way past his intelligence."

The late Senator Sam J. Ervin, Jr.
MORGANTON, NORTH CAROLINA

Possession

"Repetition is very important," said the professor. "Repeat any word twenty-five times, and it will be yours for life."

In the back of the classroom, a coed closed her eyes and said, "Henry, Henry, Henry…"

Opal Smith
LOUISVILLE, KENTUCKY

I'm with You

A new teacher, trying to make use of her psychology courses, started her class by saying, "Everyone who thinks you're stupid, stand up."

After a few seconds, little Johnny stood up. The teacher said, "Do you think you're stupid, Johnny?"

"No, ma'am," he said, "but I hate to see you standing up there all by yourself."

Loyal Jones

They Were More Tolerant

There was a college professor who hated for his students to be late to class. It was just after World War II, and about ten minutes after the lecture had started, an Air Force dischargee came in, walked all the way to the front and sat down.

The professor stopped his lecture and said to him, "What would they have said in the Air Force if you came to a lecture ten minutes late?"

The student said, "They would have all stood up, saluted,

and said, 'Good morning, Colonel. We hope you had a good night's sleep!'"

John Ed McConnell
LOUISVILLE, KENTUCKY

Not All There

The president of a great university was also a much sought-after speaker. Once he and his wife were on an airplane going to one of his speaking engagements, and he was rehearsing his speech, sitting there with his eyes closed reciting a passage he wanted to be memorable.

A woman across the aisle had been observing him, and she leaned across, patted his wife's hand and said, "You have my profound sympathy. I have one just like him at home."

Loyal Jones

"I Was Feeling Kind of Big about Myself"

P E O P L E   A T   W O R K

The Clincher

I met a young man some time ago who stuttered terribly, but he sold Bibles, sold more Bibles than anyone in his group. So, they had a meeting and asked him to tell the rest how he sold so many Bibles.

He said, "W-w-well, I j-j-j-ust t-t-tell you how I s-sell Buh-Buh-B-Buh-Bibles. I-I-I just s-s-say, w-w-wouldn't y-you l-l-like to b-buy a B-Bible? It t-t-tells here about Eve wuh-wuh-w-wearing a f-fig l-leaf. And it t-tells about M-M-M-Moses, who w-was the f-f-first man to b-break the T-T-Ten C-Commandments. Then it t-tells about S-Solomon, the s-smartest m-m-m-man in the w-world, b-but nuh-nuh-n-no wonder, h-he h-had a thousand w-w-women b-bringing him the n-n-news every d-day. Then over h-here i-it t-tells about J-Joseph, w-who was s-sold into s-slavery. H-he w-was the o-one who w-wore the D-Dolly P-Parton coat. Then it t-tells y-you about J-J-John the B-Baptist who l-l-lost his h-head over a d-dancing girl. Then the up-up-uh-Apostle Puh-P-P-

75

Puh-Paul, who was afraid t-to g-get m-m-married for f-f-fear he'd geh-g-get heartburn.

"Th-th-then, I s-s-s...ay, 'Woo-W-Woo-Would, you l-l-like t-t-to b-buy a Buh-Buh-B-Bible, or w-w-ould y-you j-just l-l-like f-for m-me t-to ree-ree-r-read it tuh-tuh-t-to you?'"

Bonnie Collins
WEST UNION,WEST VIRGINIA

Another Stutterer

This fellow got into a cab and said. "T-t-t-take m-me t-t-to the r-r-radio st-st-station."

The driver said, "What are you going to do there?"

He said, "I-I-I'm g-g-goin' to t-t-try out f-f-for a r-r-radio an-n-nnouncer."

He told the driver to wait, went up and came back in a few minutes and said, "L-l-et's g-g-get out of h-h-here."

The driver said, "I take it you didn't get the job?"

The man said, "S-s-same old st-st-story. They d-d-don't luh-luh-l-l-like hillbillies."

Billy Edd Wheeler

Whole Bunch

The boss of a construction job ran an errand, and when he came back, he found his men all sitting around. He flew mad and said, " You lazy SOBs, get up and get to work!"

All of them went back to work except one man, who said, "Boy, there was a bunch of them, wasn't there?"

Tom Ambrose
FRANKFORT, KENTUCKY

There It Is

A city fellow was conversing with a farmer and asked him what time he went to work each morning. The farmer replied, "I don't go to work. I just get up and I'm surrounded by it!"

Loyal Jones

Papal Inquiry

We have this barber in our neighborhood who is really pessimistic. He had a guy in his chair one day who said, "I won a trip. I'm going to Italy."

The barber said, "Why do you want to go to Italy? You won't like it. The people are dirty, the food isn't any good, and the whole place is run down."

The customer said, "But I'll get to see the Pope."

The barber said, "I'll tell you about that Pope business. He'll be way up there on a balcony, and you'll be back here with a whole lot of people. That's as close as you'll get to seeing the Pope."

The customer said, "I'll get to see the Pope."

He went on his trip and was gone for two weeks. When he came back, the barber said, "Well, how was it?"

The man said, "You were wrong about Italy. The people were beautiful, the country was beautiful, and the food was delicious."

"Yeah, but did you get to see the Pope?"

The man said, "Well, you were about half-right about that. The Pope was up there on the balcony and I was back here in a crowd of thousands of people, but two men showed up and told me the Pope wanted to see me to talk to me, and they took me right up there on the balcony with him."

"Well, well, what did he tell you?" asked the barber.

"He didn't tell me anything."

"Well, what did he ask you?"

"He just wanted to know where I got this God-awful haircut!"

Bonnie Collins
WEST UNION, WEST VIRGINIA

A Point Here, a Point There

The engineer standing on the bank watching a bridge go down the river said, "I always did think I got that decimal in the wrong place."

Guy Pendleton

ROANOKE, VIRGINIA

How Good Was He?

A timber company sent out word that they needed woodsmen. A man came in and said that he was the best woodchopper in the world. They had him do a demonstration, and he was pretty fast. So they asked him where he had worked last.

"Ever hear of the Sahara Forest?" he asked.

Joe Kuczko

WISE, VIRGINIA

You Ain't Seen Mad

A man got on the train in Chicago and looked up the head porter. He handed him a fifty-dollar bill and said, "Now, I'm going into my berth to get some sleep, but I want you to make sure to get me up so I can get off the train in Cincinnati." He went on to say, "I'm a very sound sleeper, and I'm hard to get up in the morning, but I'm giving you this money to make sure you get me up. Tomorrow, I'm marrying the boss's daughter in Cincinnati. It's the most important day of my life, and I have to be there."

So he went to bed, and when he woke up, he was in Louisville. Well, he was mad! He went looking for the porter, cussed him out and said, "This is the maddest I've ever been! I'm so mad I could kill you!"

The porter said, "You think *you're* mad. You should have seen the fellow I put off in Cincinnati!"

Tom T. Hall

FRANKLIN, TENNESSEE

Me and Ma Bell

When I first decided to become a professional speaker, I was feeling kind of big about myself, and that's when I learned to laugh at myself. I like to keep life, especially the humanity of us all, in perspective.

I wanted to be a professional speaker, so I set up an office in my home and started contacting executives in the big corporations and associations. Then I called the telephone company and told the lady I wanted to be listed under *Speaker*, but she said, "We don't have that category. You'll have to be listed under *Bureau* or *Lecturer*."

I said, "There ain't nobody going to hire me under *Bureau*. I want to be listed under *Speaker*."

She said, "We don't have that category."

I said, "You can *make* a category!"

She said, "I don't *make* the categories, I just put people *in* the categories!"

I said, "I want to speak to your boss, the district manager of Southern Bell."

Now, sometimes you have to go all the way to the top to get something done. You have to get tough.

So now, if you want a professional speaker, just look in the yellow pages under *Stereo Equipment*, and you'll find me right there.

Joe Bly
ASHEVILLE, NORTH CAROLINA

Better Odds

This insuranceman who traveled by air a lot, called in his actuarial people and asked, "What are the odds that I will be on an airplane that has a bomb on it?"

They went off and studied the problem and came back to tell him that his chances were fifty thousand to one. He said, "That's not good enough. Go back and figure how I can get better odds."

So they went off and studied the problem all over again and came back to say, "You can carry a bomb on the plane.

The chances of two bombs being on the same plane are a million to one."

LONDON, KENTUCKY

Bad Wreck

A policeman over in Pikeville, Kentucky, told me about this wreck he came up on—thought it was the worst one he'd ever seen. It was a Volkswagen, windshield cracked, with red stuff all over it and running everywhere. He said it turned his stomach something awful.

He really hated to go over there and open that car door. He said he walked up and reached for the door, and it swung open! This hippie got out and sort of staggered around, groggy and everything. The policeman asked him, "Are you all right?"

"Yep," he said, "I'm fine, but this pizza is a mess!"

Bob Hannah

ATLANTA, GEORGIA

Whatever Pleases

I went to the grocery store to buy some things, and being mindful of the environment, I asked for paper rather then plastic bags.

"Different pokes for different folks," said the bag boy.

Jan Davidson

CULLOWHEE, NORTH CAROLINA

See?

One time, a woman was taking a shower, and as she was drying off, the doorbell rang.

"Who is it?" she called.

"The blind man," said a voice from the other side of the door.

Obviously a person asking for a donation, she thought, so she got a dollar and opened the door, not thinking it was necessary to do more than drape the towel around her.

The man looked somewhat surprised, and asked, "OK, lady, where do I put the blinds?"

Mystery Shopper

I live in Tennessee now, but I was born up in Wolfe County, Kentucky, about sixty miles southeast of Lexington. As a young boy, I worked in a general merchandise store back in the early '40s. We kept a ledger there, and when somebody bought something on credit, we'd write it down in that ledger. They'd usually come in about once a month and pay up.

This new family moved into town, and one day the lady came into the store. I was the only one there at the time, and I couldn't remember her name to write it down on the ledger and hated to ask her, so as she left the store I called, "Well, who's that for?"

As she went out the door, she said, "It's for all of us," and just kept on going.

Dick Williams
KINGSTON, TENNESSEE

The Hometown Store

In Lakemont, Georgia, Alley's Grocery Store is a wonderful country store and the owner, Lamar Alley, sits in the window greeting people as they come and go. He's the kind of guy who always has a good word for you and tries his best to please, even when he doesn't have what you want.

A big Lincoln stopped there the other day with an Illinois license plate, and this guy came strutting into the store and asked Lamar if he had any pepperoni pizza. Lamar looked at the man, said eagerly, "No, but I've *heard* of it!"

The first time I went into Alley's Grocery Store, there was salt all over the store. It was stacked everywhere you looked.

I told Lamar, "Man, I never saw so much salt. By golly, you must sell a lot of it."

Lamar said, "You should have been in here last week. There was a fellow here that *really* knew how to sell salt!"

Bob Hannah

ATLANTA, GEORGIA

Ought To Be Good

I've got a friend named Cletis, and he's not the best educated boy that ever lived. He decided one day he wanted to work for the railroad, so he went tearing off down to the railroad yard. The man down there knew him and said, "What'cha need, Cletis?"

"Well," said Cletis, "I'd kinda like to go to work for you, maybe one of them flagging jobs."

The man said, "OK, but we'd need to give you a test."

Cletis said, "All right."

The man asked Cletis, "What would you do if there was a train coming down that way just a-flying?"

Cletis said, "I'd just get out there with that red flag and wave it."

The man said, "Can't do that, it's at night."

Cletis said, "I'd get out there with my red light and wave it."

The man said, "Can't do that, you're out of coal oil."

"Well," Cletis said, "then I'd call my sister."

The man asked, "What would you call your sister for?"

Cletis said, "I'd call my sister and tell her to come down here and see the dog-gondest wreck she's ever seen in her life!"

Ernest Cantrell

MEMPHIS, TENNESSEE

Career Choice

My friend Cletis's wife, Lucinda, is quite a churchgoer. I believe she's in church every time the door swings open.

They had a boy named Little Leon, and he'd been hanging around down the street where they were building old Mr. Seymore's house.

Leon came in one night and said at the table, "Pass the dang-goned tomatoes."

His mom said, "Leon, don't talk that way."

Directly, Little Leon said, "Pass the dad-burned taters."

His mom said, "Leon, you go out and get me a switch."

He said, "Momma, I'm a dad-gummed carpenter. If you want a switch, you're gonna have to call in an electrician!"

Ernest Cantrell

MEMPHIS, TENNESSEE

Lazy Man's Lament

My friend Cletis had a brother named Clovis. Clovis was lazy. You've never seen a hound dog that was any lazier in your life.

The boys decided they's tired of working for Clovis and him getting the good out of it without putting out any effort, so they decided they would just bury him. They loaded him in the wagon and started up toward the cemetery. Here come Sam down the road with a load of corn in the other direction, and he stopped and said, "Watcha doin', boys?"

"Well," they said, "we're going to take Clovis down to the cemetery and bury him. He ain't fit to stay around any longer."

The man said, "Clovis, I've got a nice load of corn here. Just to keep you from getting buried, I'll give it to you."

Clovis raised up and peeked over the edge of the wagon. Said, "Is it shelled, Sam?"

Sam said, "No, it ain't shelled."

Clovis said, "Drive on, boys!"

Ernest Cantrell

MEMPHIS, TENNESSEE

A Hard Sale

I used to sell hearing aids from door-to-door. It didn't work out too well, as most of my best prospects never answered the door.

Brian McFarland

ONTARIO, CANADA

83

"Stir Up Much Strife amongst the People, Lord"

T H E   L A W   A N D   P O L I T I C S

We've Tried

A fellow with legal problems came into town in a hurry and inquired of the first person he saw, "Do you have any criminal lawyers here?"

The man replied, "Yes, three or four, but we've never been able to convict any of them yet."

Dr. Charles Harris
BEREA, KENTUCKY

No Noticeable Inferiority Complex

When Teddy Roosevelt ran on the Bull Moose ticket in 1912, he made a brief back-platform campaign in Kentucky. At one station, as the train pulled out and the crowd dispersed, only an old man remained on the station platform when a latecomer arrived and inquired, "Who made the speech?"

The old man replied, "I don't know, but he shore spoke awful well of hisself!"

The late Dr. Eslie Asbury
CARLISLE, KENTUCKY

Practical Woman

A man was sent to the penitentiary for stealing hams. After a year, the man's wife went to the Governor for a pardon.

"Is he a good worker?"

"No, Governor, he's a mite trifling."

"Does he go to church?"

"No, he never sets foot in a church."

"Does he run around with other women?"

"Yes, Governor, I'm sorry to say that he does."

"Then why do you want him out?"

"I'll be honest, Governor. We're getting short of hams."

The late Dr. Eslie Asbury
CARLISLE, KENTUCKY

Needed Help

There was a young lawyer who showed up at a revival meeting and was asked to deliver a prayer. Unprepared, he gave a prayer straight from his lawyer's heart: "Stir up much strife amongst the people, Lord," he prayed, "lest thy servant perish."

The late Senator Sam J. Ervin, Jr.
MORGANTOWN, NORTH CAROLINA

I'll Be Darned

A while ago there were three lawyers together, and one of them bet another five dollars that he did not know the Lord's Prayer. So each one put up five dollars with the third one.

Then they called on the challenged lawyer to recite the Lord's Prayer, and he said, "Now I lay me down to sleep...."

The other lawyer said, "Go ahead. Pay him off. I didn't think he knew it."

The late Senator Sam J. Ervin, Jr.
MORGANTOWN, NORTH CAROLINA

Are You Kidding?

"Do you swear to tell the truth, the whole truth, and nothing but the truth, so help you God?" the bailiff asked a witness in swearing him in.

"If I could tell the truth, the whole truth, and nothing but the truth," the witness responded, "I would *be* God!"

Dr. Donald Graham
BEREA, KENTUCKY

Another Lawyer

There was this lawyer who went camping with his non-lawyer friend. They had on their backpacks, and they saw this cougar about twenty yards up ahead. The lawyer started taking off his pack.

"What are you doing?" his friend asked.

"I'm going to run for it," the lawyer said.

"But you can't outrun a cougar," said his friend.

"I don't have to outrun the cougar," said the lawyer. "I just have to outrun you."

Dr. Jim W. Miller
BOWLING GREEN, KENTUCKY

Experimental Animals

"Do you know that scientists are now using lawyers and politicians instead of rats in their laboratory experiment?"

"No. Why?"

"Well, first, because there are more of them than there are rats; second, you don't get as attached to them as you do rats; and third, they'll do things that rats won't do."

Dr. Jim W. Miller
BOWLING GREEN, KENTUCKY

More Lawyers

It was late on Friday during a court term when the judge was presented with a commitment case. He sent the sheriff out into the corridors to round up twelve jurors for a quick decision. The sheriff came back and said all he could find at that hour were lawyers. So the judge had him bring in twelve, and he swore them in.

The evidence presented was quick and to the point. The object of the case was clearly out of control and a menace to himself, his family, and society. The jury was asked to retire and decide the case. The judge went back to his chambers, took off his robe, and got ready to go home for the weekend.

He waited for an hour, and then two hours, fidgeting and restless. Finally he sent for the sheriff to go bring the jury in to see what the problem was. When they filed in and were seated, he asked if they had come to a decision.

One of them said, "Well, we haven't got to the evidence yet. We're still making nominating speeches to see who will be foreman."

Judge William Jennings
RICHMOND, KENTUCKY

Total

Alf Landon, who won only two states against Roosevelt in 1936, retained a sense of humor in defeat. He said it reminded him of a Kansas farmer who lost his house, barn, fences, and livestock in a tornado, and who laughed.

His wife asked him why, and he said, "It's just the completeness of it."

Loyal Jones

Mighty Generous

A fellow was up before the judge for non-support of a wife and six children. The judge listened to all the evidence and then said, "You just haven't done right by your wife and children. I'll tell you what I'm going to do. I'm going to give them two hundred dollars a month."

The defendent looked pleased, smiled, and said, "Why thank you, Judge, and I'll chip in a few dollars myself when I can afford it."

Loyal Jones

Amateur

My uncle Vern Smith was in the Virginia legislature, and as a teenager, my dad's job was to drive him to the legislature. Vern was bad to play poker, and one night he had a bunch of men in the old Jefferson Hotel in Richmond playing poker, and my father was there, too. They all got to drinking a considerable amount of whiskey.

Next morning, my father woke up with a terrible hangover. He had heard of the hair of the dog that bit you, so he reached over and got a bottle of Jack Daniels and took a swig and threw up.

At that point, Uncle Vern sat up in bed and said, "Ernest, if you're just practicing, I wish you'd use that other cheap whiskey."

Lee Smith

CHAPEL HILL, NORTH CAROLINA

One-Track Mind

When Abraham Lincoln was practicing law, his client was opposed by an attorney known for his oratory, which was sometimes devoid of logic. When Lincoln addressed the jury he said:

> My friend on the other side is all right, or would be all right, were it not for the peculiarity I am about to chronicle. His habit...of reckless assertion and statements without grounds need not be imputed to him as a moral fault or as telling of moral blemish. He can't help it....The moment he begins to talk, his mental operations cease. I never knew of but one thing which compared with my friend in this particular. That was a small steam-

boat. Back in the days when I performed my part as a keel-boat man, I made the acquaintance of a trifling little steamboat which used to bustle and puff and wheeze about the Sangamon River. It had a five-foot boiler and a seven-foot whistle, and every time it whistled, it stopped.

Those Isms

A candidate for the Senate was waxing pretty eloquent on the evils of leftist politics to a rural audience. He shouted at the top of his lungs, "We've got to get rid of all these threats to our way of life. I mean bolshevism, socialism, communism..."

A stooped old farmer interrupted, "While you're at it, why don't you get rid of rheumatism, too?"

Loyal Jones

Not Me

Two politicians were campaigning for an office from the same platform. The first one to speak accused the second one of being illiterate.

His opponent jumped up and shouted, "That's a damn lie. My daddy and mama was married at least a year before I was born!"

Loyal Jones

Deductive Reasoning

A fellow over in Frankfort many years ago killed a hog during a term of the legislature, scraped and cleaned it, cut it in half, and hung the two sides in his smokehouse to cool. During the night, someone stole one of the halves.

He went tearing down to the capitol and accused the Republicans of the theft. One of the Republican legislators took issue with him.

"How do you know it was a Republican?" he demanded.

"Because a Democrat would have taken both halves," the man retorted.

John Ed McConnell
LOUISVILLE, KENTUCKY

Frugal

Of a rival: "He has a great respect for the truth. That is why he uses it so sparingly."

Joe Palmer
LEXINGTON, KENTUCKY

Tact

Lawyer Stowers, of Pikeville, Kentucky, was a born diplomat and a suave gentleman. One day a lady accompanied by a poodle dog met him on the street, and they began to chat. In a little while the dog walked over and began to smell Stower's legs. Then he started to raise a hind paw to perform a very common canine function. Stowers jumped back out of the way.

"Oh, Mr. Stowers, I'm so sorry."

"Never mind. I thought he was going to kick me."

The late Dr. Josiah H. Combs
FORT WORTH, TEXAS

A Clipboard Constable Keeps Count

I live about eighteen miles northeast of Knoxville, Tennessee, up there on the Union County line. There are places there like Big Tater Valley, Little Tater Valley, Pumpkin Hollow, and Toad Town. Up around Luttrell, Tennessee— that's where Chet Atkins was born—an old boy by the name of J.T. Atkins decided to run for constable.

Well, old J.T. went down to the courthouse, got a list of all qualified voters in his district, put them on a clipboard, got in his pickup truck, and started out on the backroads to do a little electioneering.

He come up on this widow woman's house, knocked on her door, and told her he was running for constable and would she vote for him?

She said, "J.T. Atkins, I wouldn't vote for you if you was the last man on earth. You're a drunk, been in jail, ran off and left your wife, and you beat your kids. I just wouldn't vote for you a-tall!"

Well, J.T. went back to his truck, got out his clipboard and found her name, and wrote "doubtful."

Jesse Butcher

UNION COUNTY, TENNESSEE

The Power of Negative Thinking

I've got to tell you one about Willie Thorp. Willie lives back there in Little Tater Valley, and he was working at Oak Ridge when he got laid off. He decided to go squirrel hunting. Well, it had come a big heavy rain while he was out hunting, and he was without shelter, so he crawled up into a big hollow log and went to sleep. The rain kept coming down, and that log swole up so that old Willie couldn't get out! So he shot every shell he had, dug and clawed trying to get out, and he decided that he was going to die right here in that log.

All at once, everything he'd ever done wrong flashed right in front of his mind, and he happened to think that at one time he'd voted for Ronald Reagan. It made him feel so little, he shrunk up and crawled right on out of there!

Jesse Butcher

UNION COUNTY, TENNESSEE

The Mule and the Foxhounds

I've just got to tell you about old Cleve Melderbar's mule. Nearly everybody down there in Union County keeps an old mule around just to plow out a little patch of tobacco or plow out the garden.

Well, old Cleve passed on and left an old mule there named John. John was worried about Cleve and missed him

92

a lot, so he got sick. So, Mrs. Melderbar got on the phone and called Joe Smelter, the local veterinarian. She told Joe she wanted him to come out and see old John, who was sick and laying down in the stall, groaning and going on.

He said, "Bertha, I've been out *all* day, and I'm dead tired. What I want you to do is go out there and give old John a dose of mineral oil. You got any?"

She said, "Yep. How do I give it to him?"

"Well," he said, "pour it down him if you can, but if you can't, get a funnel." He said he'd be out to see John in the morning. He felt sure he'd be all right and told her not to worry.

So she went out to the barn, and old John was laying down there in that stall, his eyes closed, and he's groaning and goin' on and all. She couldn't get old John to take that mineral oil down his mouth. The Doc had told her to use a funnel if she had to, but she couldn't find one. She looked around and found a fox horn hanging up there and, you know, these horns have a great big knob on them, where you blow.

Well, the Doc had told her to raise his tail, if she couldn't get it into his mouth, just as long as she got the mineral oil into him someway. So she raised his tail and shoved that fox horn right in as far as she could get it, and reached for the mineral oil. But it happened to be *turpentine!* She poured that bottle of turpentine into old John, and he laid there a minute. Then them eyes flew open, them ears come up, and he jumped up and took both hind feet and kicked that stall door open. Down that hallway John went, through the barnyard, and jumped the gate. Everytime he'd kick, he'd break a little wind and blow that horn! Well, Bertha's neighbor Redeye Thorp is a foxhunter and he had a lot of foxhounds. They heard old John a-blowing that horn, a-kicking and breakin' that wind, so they thought a chase was on!

Them dogs jumped out of that dog lot and took off down that dirt road after old John! He was a-kicking, breaking wind, and a-blowing that horn. And them hounds was a-barking and going on. They come right down to the river.

Leslie Graves was operating a toll bridge down there, one of them bridges that you raise up to let boats go through, you know. Well, he was asleep, and when he heard that ruckus a-coming, he thought it was a boat. So the first thing he done was raise the bridge! Well, old John went right up over the bridge, down into the water with them dogs, and drowned!

Mrs. Melderbar got real mad about it. Leslie was a-running for sheriff, so she decided she'd get out and campaign against him. She said if he'd left that bridge down, old John would have soon run out of gas!

You know, old Leslie lost that election by a *wide* margin, 'cause the people in that county figured if he didn't know the difference between a steamboat coming up the river and a mule breaking wind, then he didn't have enough sense to be sheriff of the county!

Jesse Butcher
UNION COUNTY, TENNESSEE

And They'd Be Running

"If God had meant for us to have elections, he would have given us candidates."

Dr. Bill Foster
FLORENCE, ALABAMA

"Our Father, Did You See That?"

PREACHERS, CHURCHES, AND RELIGION

Ruining Hell

Oral Roberts, Jim Bakker, and Jimmy Swaggart all died and went to the Pearly Gates. They knocked, and St. Peter came with his book. One of them said, "Open up, we've arrived."

St. Peter looked in his book and said, "You fellows are mistaken. According to my book, you are supposed to go to the other place."

Well, they were pretty upset over this and argued that they were all preachers and had done great works on earth, but St. Peter got on the phone and called the Devil, who said to send them on down because he had been expecting them. So they went off to Hell, pretty mad and disappointed.

About a week later, St. Peter got a call from the Devil, who said, "I'm sending those three fellows back up to you. I can't have them down here. They've already raised enough money to air condition Hell."

Josh Fuller
JEFFERSON CITY, MISSOURI

Get Him Ready, Lord: A Prayer

Oh, Lord, give Brother Jones the eye of an eagle, so that he may see sin from afar; luminate his brow with a brightness that will make the fires of Hell look like a tallow candle; glue his ears to the Gospel telephone that connects him to the heavenly skies; nail his hands to the pulpit plow and bow his head down in some lonesome valley where prayer is wont to be said; pizen his mind with the love of the people; turpentine his imagination; grease his lips with 'possum oil; electrify his brain with the lightning of the Word; loosen his tongue with the sledge hammer of Thy power; put perpetual motion in his arms; fill him with glory; anoint him all over with the kerosene oil of Thy salvation, *and set him on fire!*

Bob Hannah
ATLANTA, GEORGIA

Waiting in Line

Three women arrived at the Pearly Gates at the same time. St. Peter came but said he had some pressing business and would they please wait. He was gone a long time, but finally he came back and called one of the women in and asked her if she minded waiting.

"No," she said, "I've looked forward to this for so long. I love God and I can't wait to meet Jesus. I don't mind at all."

St. Peter then said, "Well, I have one more question. How do you spell 'God'?"

She said, "Capital-G-o-d."

St. Peter said, "Go right on in."

He went out and got one of the other women, told her to come on inside, said, "Did you mind waiting?"

She said, "Oh, no. I have been a Christian for fifty years, and I'll spend eternity here. I didn't mind at all."

96

So St. Peter said, "Just one more thing. How do you spell 'God'?"

She said, "G-o-d. No, I mean *capital*-G."

St. Peter said that was good and sent her on in to Heaven.

He went back out and invited the third woman in and asked her if she minded waiting.

"Yes, I did," she said. "I've had to stand in line all my life—at the supermarket, when I went to school, when I registered my children for school, when I went to the movies—everywhere—and I resent having to wait in line for Heaven!"

St. Peter said, "Well, that's all right for you to feel that way. It won't be held against you, but there is just one more question. How do you spell 'Czechoslovakia'?"

The Rev. Patrick Napier

BEREA, KENTUCKY

Uncollared

A priest went on vacation to a little resort town. A local fellow engaged him in conversation, and when he found he was a priest, he said, "My lay church group is having a meeting tonight, and we'd love to have you speak to us."

The priest said he would but then remembered that he had not brought a clerical collar with him. So he went to the local priest, explained his situation and asked if he might borrow a collar.

The other priest nodded and said, "I understand your situation: a lay date and a collar short."

Dr. Richard Barnes

BEREA, KENTUCKY

Enough is Enough

My folks came from Ireland. My father wasn't Catholic, but there were fifteen of us kids. He was sexy-Protestant.

The Irish thought they ought to have many children. John and Mary Murphy got married but didn't have any

97

children right away. They talked to their priest about it, and he said, "Oh, I'm going to Rome, and I'll light a candle for ye."

He left and went to Rome, but they transferred him to another parish, and he didn't come back for ten or twelve years. When he came back, the Murphys had twelve kids, and she was pregnant again!

He said to Mrs. Murphy, "I want to congratulate ye, and I want to congratulate your husband, John. Where is he?"

She said, "Father, you won't be able to see him for a long time. He's in Rome trying to blow out that bloody candle!"

Bonnie Collins
WEST UNION, WEST VIRGINIA

Another Miracle

An old woman at the customs office was asked if she had anything to declare.

"No, nothing at all."

"But what's in this bottle?" the customs agent asked.

"Oh, only holy water from Lourdes."

The customs officer pulled the cork.

"Whiskey, it is," he said.

"Glory be to God," cried the old lady, "another miracle!"

John Ed McConnell
LOUSIVILLE, KENTUCKY

Getting Away From It

There was this Jewish boy who went away to college, and when he came home, his mother said to him, "Well, Sammie..."

The boy said, "Just stop right there. My name is Sam. I'm a man now."

She said, "Well, I just wanted to know if you still go to the temple to pray for your soul?"

He said, "No, I don't. I'm through with old-world religion!"

"Well," said his mother, "don't you still eat kosher food?"

He said, "No, Mother, I don't eat kosher food. I don't go to the temple or anything," he said.

"Just one more question, Sammie," she said. "Are you still circumcised?"

Bonnie Collins
WEST UNION, WEST VIRGINIA

Real Bright

I knew this fellow who went to the seminary. He was brilliant, was first in his class, Phi Beta Kappa, about as bright as anybody who'd ever graduated from the seminary, but he had one failing. He couldn't remember names. So he had to have these cheat cards in his coat pocket.

He got up to preach his first sermon, looked out over the congregation, and started to preach. "In the beginning..." he reached in his pocket for a card, looked at it, "...*God* created Heaven and earth. He made the first man..." looked at the card, "...*Adam,* and the first woman..." looked at the card, "...*Eve.* And from this union begat the first child..." He reached for another card, pulled back his coat, couldn't find a card and said, "...*Kuppenheimer.*"

Bob Hannah
ATLANTA, GEORGIA

A Preacher's Inspiration

You know, Baptist people can ordain each other. You can even be ordained on Saturday and preach on Sunday. But the Methodists do it a little different; they've got these seminars, and they take these young boys and teach 'em whatever and place them in these small churches around in the various communities.

Well, one old boy graduated from one of those seminars, and he was a dead ringer for Conway Twitty. I mean a *dead ringer!* So, he looked over the ledger there, looked over the names of his flock and decided to visit some of the members of the congregation. He went down to this woman's house and knocked on the door.

When she opened the door, she exclaimed, "Conway Twitty!"

And he said, "No, ma'am, I'm your new pastor, and I wanted to stop by and have a prayer with you."

So she said come right on in.

He done that a couple of times down the street there, and everyone thought he was Conway Twitty.

Then he come to a widow woman's house on the end of the street. She was in taking a shower. Her neighbor had promised her a cake recipe, and she was expecting Mildred to come by and bring it anytime. So, the doorbell rang, and she was in there singing along a little bit and taking that shower, and all she did was fling a towel around her shoulders and run to the door and open it.

She said, "Well, Conway Twitty!"

And he said, "Hello, darlin'!"

Jesse Butcher
UNION COUNTY, TENNESSEE

Auspicious Entry

This is *supposed* to be a true story, one I learned when I was in the seminary.

There was this young minister who had just graduated from the seminary with a Ph.D., and his dissertation had not even begun collecting dust yet on the back shelf of the library.

He'd been called to this country church where he was going to lead them in high church liturgy. They were kind-hearted people, generous and decent, and they didn't want to interfere with his new-fangled ideas too much. So they were trying to go along with him.

He had worked out a *processional*, one of those *processionals* that you write out in italics in the bulletins. In this *processional*, the choir would come into the church first, singing the Doxology, and he would trail in after them, arriving at the pulpit just as the choir had concluded the Doxology.

He had bought a new robe, and it was a bit long, and he got his long robe tangled up somehow, and he just fell flat on his face in front of everybody—God and the whole church. You know what happens, the children begin to twitter and laugh first, then the young people, then the old folks join in.

The minister gets to the pulpit at last and sees that everybody is about to crack up, that they can hardly hold it back. He thinks, "I'd better not pray myself—who can I call on?"

He looks at a brother whose face is always turpentine and quinine—he hasn't smiled in about a year. The minister thinks he is safe in calling on him to lead the opening prayer. He says, "Brother Smith, would you lead our invocation?"

And Brother Smith says, "Our Father, did you see that? *Haw...Haw...Haw...*"

Dr. Lee Morris
BEREA, KENTUCKY

So Here I Am

I'm not a member of any organized religious group. I'm a Methodist. I would have been a Presbyterian, but I didn't have a gray suit.

Joe Bly
ASHEVILLE, NORTH CAROLINA

Under Cover

A friend of mine was in front of me coming out of church one day, and the preacher was standing at the door as he always is to shake hands. He grabbed my friend by the hand and pulled him aside.

He said, "You need to join the Army of the Lord!"

My friend said, "I'm already in the Army of the Lord, Pastor."

The pastor said, "How come I don't see you except at Christmas and Easter?"

He whispered back, "I'm in the secret service."

Joe Bly
ASHEVILLE, NORTH CAROLINA

Just Beautiful

A man and his wife were sitting in church one evening. His wife was listening to the choir singing, but her husband's mind had wandered and he was listening to the katydids sing just outside the window.

When the choir finished, she said, "Wasn't that just beautiful?"

And he said, "Yes, and they say they do that by rubbing their legs together."

Vertie Mintz
MARBLE, NORTH CAROLINA,
as told by her grandfather
The Rev. Francis Marion Morgan,
FLATS, NORTH CAROLINA

Humble Prayer

"Lord, help me to believe and accept the truth about myself, no matter how beautiful it is."

The Rev. Joseph Mark Newcomer
BILLINGS, MONTANA

Good Hand

There was this fellow who had been pretty sinful most of his life, and he went to this little Baptist church down the road. He decided that he would get baptized and join the church. His wife was a little skeptical about the whole thing.

The preacher took him out to the river, and his wife and son went along. When the preacher dunked him, a deck of cards came floating up. And you know what? The ace of spades came floating up around his head, and then the king, the queen, the jack, and then the ten!

His wife hollered, "Oh Lord, Preacher, he's lost!"

But his son said, "No, Mama, with a hand like that, he can be saved!"

Paul Lepp
SOUTH CHARLESTON, WEST VIRGINIA

No Way

A Sunday School teacher had just finished telling her class about Noah and the Ark. She asked, "Now how do you think Noah spent his time while they were on the ark?"

A litle girl held up her hand and said, "I'll bet he fished a lot."

A little boy said, "How could he? He only had two worms."

Loyal Jones

Preparation

There was a legendary preacher named Brother Patterson who was called to minister a church in the mountains near Elizabethton, Tennessee, years ago. The church had been terrorized by a local tough who would get drunk and disturb services. In his first sermon, Brother Patterson denounced the bully by name.

The two met on the road the next day, and the tough said he was going to beat up the preacher. Brother Patterson said he would accommodate him, but he would like a few moments to pray in preparation.

He began, "O Lord, thou knowest that when I was forced to kill Bill Cummins and John Brown and Jerry Smith and Levi Bottles, I did it in self-defense. Thou knowest that when I cut the heart out of young Slinger and strewed the ground with the brains of Paddy Miles, it was forced on me, and I did it with great agony of soul.

"And now, O Lord, I am forced to put in his coffin this poor, miserable wretch. Have mercy on his soul and take care of his widow and his orphans."

Brother Patterson rose, took his knife from his pocket and began to whet it on a stone, and sang in a loud voice, "Hark, from the tomb a dolesome sound, mine ears attend the cry!"

When he looked around, the tough had disappeared.

Don Seabrook
NEW ALBANY, INDIANA

Epitaph

When I die, bury me deep,
Put a jug of molasses at my feet,
Put two biscuits in my hand,
And I'll sop my way to the promised land.

Dr. Louis Smith

BEREA, KENTUCKY

Enlightened

A Baptist preacher had some pups for sale, and advertised them in the local newspaper under the headline, "Methodist Pups For Sale." After a while a man came and asked to see them. He didn't like the price, so he went away. A few days later he came back and said he would take one of the Methodist pups.

The preacher said, "They're Baptist pups now."

The man inquired how that had come to be, and the preacher replied, "They've got their eyes open."

The Rev. John Sherfey

STANLEY, VIRGINIA

Just What He Wanted

Two fellows were called to Heaven, but when they got to the Pearly Gates, St. Peter met them and said, "Oh dear, there's been a mistake. You weren't supposed to be here for two more weeks." He stood around thinking and finally said, "Look, would you be interested in going back to earth for a while? You can't go back as your old selves, but you can be anything you want to be for two weeks."

The first one said, "You know, I love eagles. I've always wished I was an eagle. Could I go back as one?"

Quick as a flash he was gone.

The second one said, "Well, I don't know whether I ought to say this or not. I'm sure you won't approve, but I've always wanted to be a stud."

Pfffft! He was gone.

In two weeks, St. Peter called in one of his angels. Said, "You remember those two guys we had up here two weeks ago we weren't ready for? I need you to go get them now."

The angel asked where he might find them.

St. Peter said, "If you go to the Grand Canyon, you'll find the first one soaring around the place as an eagle."

The angel said that was fine and asked about the other one.

St. Peter said, "Well, down there just across the Tennessee line in Kentucky, right next to Interstate 75, there is a Jim Walter house. He'll be just behind the wallboard in the living room."

Jim Rickels
MT. VERNON, KENTUCKY

Space Savers

The Methodists were getting ready for their revival in this rural area, and they let it be known that they needed volunteers to keep folks who wanted to attend from the country.

A Baptist lady called up and said, "I can keep six."

"How many rooms and beds do you have?" she was asked.

"Only one," she said, "but Methodists are so narrow, I can get six in a bed."

F. B. Smith
WHEREABOUTS UNKNOWN

Advertising

A fellow went to confession in a Catholic church. He said, "Father, I have sinned. I am eighty-five years old, and I've been faithful to my wife ever since we were married sixty years ago, but last night I made mad, passionate love to eighteen-year-old twins."

The priest was somewhat taken aback, and stalling for time, he asked, "How long has it been since you came to confession?"

105

"Oh, I've never been to confession before," the man said. "I'm Baptist."

"Then why are you telling me this?" the priest asked.

"Oh, I'm telling everybody," the man said.

Loyal Jones

Oh, Well...

Another man went to confession and said, "Father, I have sinned. I have committed adultery."

The priest said, "My son, this is terrible, a major sin. For penance..."

"There's more," the man said. "We did it on the steps of the cathedral."

"Oh, dear," said the priest. "This is a great sin and also blasphemy and a desecration of the church—more serious than I thought. For penance..."

"There's more. I did it with the wife of the Episcopalian rector."

"Well," said the priest, "boys will be boys."

Bill Hastings
BEREA, KENTUCKY

Hydration

Following a revival, a baptism of the converts was being held at the lake. As a converted reprobate was being led into the water, a member on shore yelled out, "I've known this old sinner for many years. Just one dip won't do him any good, Reverend. You'll have to anchor him out in deep water overnight."

Judge Ray Corns
FRANKFORT, KENTUCKY

Rivalry

Two churches were very competetive and both erected billboards. One put up the following message:

Be sure to profess what you possess.

Next week the other church put up this message:

Be sure you possess what you profess.
Billy Wilson
BEREA, KENTUCKY

No Way

There was this little boy who cussed all the time. One day, the preacher heard him and delivered a stern warning. He said that if he didn't stop, the Boogerman would get him.

"Where is he?" the boy asked.

"He's everywhere," the preacher said.

"In Grandma's cellar?"

"Yes."

"I know that's a damn lie. Grandma ain't got no cellar!"
Dr. Billy Friar
DAYTON, OHIO

Of All the Things He Could Have Done

A fellow came to Clarksville, Georgia, and wanted to set up a winery. The city council was made up of Baptists, and they objected to the plan. So the fellow came to a meeting of the council to argue his case. He explained that the climate was good for grapes, that he could make good wine, and that it would employ a lot of people and might even be a fine tourist attraction.

A member of the council jumped up and said, "We don't believe in alcohol. If you build a winery, there'll be alcohol in that wine, and I'm against it."

The fellow said, "But you know that Jesus made wine as one of his miracles."

The councilman said, "Yes, but his wine didn't have any alcohol in it."

About this time, the mayor spoke up and said, "That argument won't wash. Wine, by its very nature has alcohol in it. I just don't know why Jesus did that—turning water into wine. All my life, that's been an embarrassment to me!"
Millard Fuller
AMERICUS, GEORGIA

Appropriate Punishment

An Episopalian died and went to Heaven. St. Peter was conducting him through Purgatory when he saw some people who were just miserable. So he asked, "Who are those people and what have they done to deserve this?"

St. Peter said, "Those are Jews, and they are guilty of eating ham."

They went on and found another group in worse shape, so the man asked who they were and what they had done. St. Peter said, "Those are Catholics, and they are guilty of eating ham on Fridays."

They went on and found a group of people much more miserable than the other two, and so he asked, "Who are these people, and what have they done that was so bad?"

"Well," said St. Peter, "those are Episcopalians, and they were caught eating ham with their salad forks."

Dr. Lee Morris

BEREA, KENTUCKY

Nothing Doing

A circuit preacher came by a mountain cabin on horseback and stopped to speak to a woman standing in the door. "Do you have any Presbyterians around here?"

"I don't think so," she said, "but my husband hunts and traps a lot of varmints, and he skins them and nails their hides to the barn wall. You can go look to see if he got one of them if you want to."

The preacher said, "I can see that you are living in darkness."

"Yes," she said, "I've been trying to get John to cut me a window in the side of the house, but I can't get him to do nothing."

"Did you know that Christ died for your sins?" the preacher persisted.

"No, I didn't," she answered. "I live up in this holler, and I don't hear nothing. I didn't even know he was sick."

The preacher said, "Well, I've got to go. I hope to meet you at the Pearly Gates."

"I won't meet no man at no gate. I met a man the other night, and John like to a killed me."

Anna Perkins

TEABERRY, KENTUCKY

Church Bloopers

Wednesday at 7:30 there will be a meeting of the Little Mothers Club. All wishing to become Little Mothers please meet with the minister in his study.

All members are invited to a potluck supper on Wednesday at 6:00. Prayer and medication will follow.

During the absence of our pastor, we enjoyed the rare privilege of hearing a good sermon when J.F. Stubbs supplied our pulpit.

Remember in prayer the many who are sick of our church and community.

Today—Christian Youth Fellowship House Sexuality Course, 8 p.m. Please park in the rear parking lot for this activity.

A bean supper will be held Saturday evening in the church basement. Music will follow.

Tuesday at 5 p.m. there will be an ice cream social. All ladies giving milk, please come early.

This being Easter, we will ask Mrs. Johnson to come forward and lay an egg on the altar.

The preacher will preach his farewell message, after which the choir will sing, "Break Forth With Joy."

The Rev. Morgan spoke briefly, much to the delight of his audience.

For those of you who have children and don't know it, we have a nursery downstairs.

The ladies of the church have cast off clothing of every kind, and they can be seen in the church basement on Friday afternoon.

This afternoon there will be a meeting in the south and north ends of the church. Children will be baptised at both ends.

The church is glad to have with us today as our guest minister the Rev. Shirley Green who has Mrs. Green with him. After the service we request that all remain in the sanctuary for the Hanging Of The Greens.

The "eighth graders" will be presenting Shakespeare's "Hamlet" in the church basement on Friday at 7 p.m. The congregation is invited to attend this tragedy.

Contributed by Dr. Oscar Rucker
and Marilyn Feldkamp, both of
BEREA, KENTUCKY

Weepy

Skeptic commenting on a prominent female TV evangelist: "I believe that woman's tear ducts are connected to her kidneys."

Phil Harris
CORBIN, KENTUCKY

A Hard Way to Go

A grandmother who was very religious took her small grandson to church one Sunday. The preacher got carried away and preached for over an hour.

The little boy squirmed on the hard pew and finally asked, "Are you sure that this is the only way to get to heaven?"

Loyal Jones

Lessening the Damage

I am a Presbyterian and have not missed Sunday School since August, 1936—not righteous, but stubborn.

Several years ago, I went to a Catholic wedding. At the reception I was enjoying a spot of bourbon with the priest. A photographer came, addressed the good father and said, "I want to take your picture."

The priest put the glass of bourbon behind his back. I said, "Are you afraid to have your picture taken with that glass of liquor in your hand?"

His reply was, "It's bad enough to have it taken standing next to a Presbyterian."

Saunders Guerrant
ROANOKE, VIRGINIA

Recognition

"You know how Jews don't recognize Christ?"

"Yeah."

"And how Unitarians don't recognize the Trinity?"

"Yeah."

"And how Baptists don't recognize one another in a liquor store?"

Hope Coulter
LITTLE ROCK, ARKANSAS

Mind Those P's

After filling out an application for employment, the young man took it up to the secretary. She said, "You didn't fill out that part about your religious preference."

He said, "Well, I'm Presbyterian, but I don't know how to spell it."

She replied, "Well, why don't you just put a 'P'?"

He said, "Good heavens, I don't want you to think I'm Piscopalian!"

Doris J. Locke
MALAKOFF, TEXAS

In a Word

I once knew this preacher back home who liked to use words that he sometimes didn't quite understand. One time he brought in a visiting preacher, and after introducing him to the congregation, he told him to preach loud, "because the agnostics in this church are not very good."

The late Senator Sam J. Ervin, Jr.
MORGANTON, NORTH CAROLINA

Scriptural

The preacher was calling on his parish members on a Saturday afternoon and rang the doorbell at one home. He rang, knocked, but no one answered. Then he heard footsteps inside. This annoyed him and he left his card and wrote on the back:

> *Rev. 3:20—"Behold I stand at the door and knock; if anyone hears my voice and opens the door, I will come in."*

On Sunday, as he stood at the church door, a woman passed and gave him her card, and on it was written:

> *Gen. 3:10, "I heard the sound of you in the garden, and I was afraid because I was naked and I hid myself."*

Marian Johnson
NORTH CANTON, OHIO

Sparse Company

A little girl had been to Sunday school, and on coming home, she seemed depressed and wouldn't play or eat and from time to time let out a big sigh. Her mother kept asking her what was wrong, but she said nothing was.

112

At last her mother said, "Honey, I know something is bothering you, so won't you tell Mama?"

"Well," the little girl said, "today in Sunday school, our teacher said that if anyone tells a lie, they can't go to heaven. Is that true, Mama?"

"Yes," said her mother. "I'm afraid it is."

The little girl took another sighing breath and said, "Well, it sure is going to be awful lonesome up in heaven with nobody there except God and George Washington."

Ed Ward

BLEDSOE, KENTUCKY

Another Miracle

Two Catholic nuns, both nurses, were on their way to call on a patient when they ran out of gas. They didn't have a can or bucket in the car, but they did have a bedpan they were taking to their patient. One of them suggested that they take the bedpan to a nearby gas station to get it filled.

This they did, and while they were pouring the gasoline into the tank, two Protestants drove by, and one of them said, "Did you see that? Pull over and park. I want to see if that car runs, and if it does, I'm going to convert!"

Marwood Goetz

TUCSON, ARIZONA

Good Ole Dogs

The old country preacher decided to preach on the Twenty-Third Psalm, and he went verse by verse, giving his understanding of the meaning of each. He did just fine until he came to the last verse, and he read, "Surely goodness and mercy shall follow me all the days of my life…"

He paused thoughtfully, and then said, "You know, the shepherds of old always had two dogs, and when they drove their sheep, one dog would be at the front of the flock and the other at the rear. Now, it occurs to me that the psalmist also had two faithful dogs whose names were Goodness and Mercy, and they followed him all the days of his life."

A true story contributed by
Karen Green Blondell
MIDDLESBORO, KENTUCKY

Vehicular Rewards

A man died and went to Heaven, and up there he waited with three other fellows, and when they were admitted, St. Peter said, "Heaven is a big place, and we issue vehicles for you to get around in, but first I have to ask you each a question: were you faithful to your wife?"

This man said, "Yes, I was. I never cheated on her."

So St. Peter said, "I'm pleased to issue you this Cadillac."

It was a beauty, and the man drove off happily.

When St. Peter asked the second man if he had been faithful, he said he'd only cheated once, so he gave him a Chevrolet Cavalier.

The third man admitted that he had cheated twice, and so he got a Volkswagen.

The guy in the Volkswagen was driving around, and he saw the man who got the Cadillac parked along one of the golden streets, and he was just crying his eyes out.

"What in the world are you crying about?" he asked. "You have this great big Cadillac, and you should be happy."

The man looked up and said, "My wife just went by on a skateboard."

Faye Holbrook
MT. VERNON, KENTUCKY
April Stinson
ALBANY, KENTUCKY

Man's Best Friend

A preacher gave an unusually short sermon one morning, and then afterwards he explained that he had prepared a thoughtful sermon for the day, but his dog had chewed it up during the night.

When he was greeting parishioners at the door after the service, a visitor stopped to inquire, "Does your dog by any chance have pups? I sure would like to buy one for my preacher."

Loyal Jones

Fair Warning

A young minister had just got out of the seminary, got his first church, and was preaching his first sermon.

He started out with a quote, "Behold I cometh..." but he couldn't remember the rest of it. In the seminary, they had told him that if he forgot something, just back up and repeat what he had said, and maybe it would come back to him.

So, he said again, "Behold I cometh..." but he still couldn't remember. So he reared back and shouted again, "Behold I cometh..." but this time, he tripped over the pulpit and fell onto a little woman sitting in the first row. He was embarrassed and started apologizing.

"It ain't your fault," the woman said. "You told me you was coming three times, and I never did move!"

Tonya Marcum and
Martha Burchett
ALBANY, KENTUCKY

Dust In or Dust Out?

A little boy comes in and says to his mother, "Is it true that we come from dust and return to dust?"

"That's what the Bible says," she answered.

"Well, somebody is either coming or going under my bed," he said.

Marilyn Feldkamp
BEREA, KENTUCKY

115

Tailor-Made

A guy went into the restroom in an airport in Atlanta one time, and as he stood there shoulder to shoulder with another guy doing their, you know, stand-up business, he looks over at the other guy and says, "I bet you're from Cincinnati, aren't you?"

The other man said, "My goodness, yes. How did you know?"

He said, "Well, I know the rabbi there, and he cuts on the bias. You're peeing in my shoe!"

Ray Stevens

NASHVILLE, TENNESSEE

Hot Dog, Jesus

When I got my education, part of it was at the seminary in Louisville, Kentucky. Later, when I was working with some young folks, I realized there was one word that I didn't know how to translate. It was *hallelujah*. I really needed some way to translate the meaning of this word to people so they could understand it better. I found out that the word in Hebrew means "praise God," but that didn't do too much for me, either.

One day, I was listening to the radio and heard a Pentecostal preacher say, "Sometimes I get so excited, I just have to r'ar back and say, 'Hot dog, *Jesus!*'" I knew that was what I was looking for, and that's where this song came from:

Well, He's the sausage of my breakfast,
The sandwich of my lunch,
The meatloaf of my supper,
He's the head of the bunch!

He's the frosting on my cake,
The ice cream on my pie,
Sweeter than the honeycomb,
The apple of my eye.

116

He's the gas that fills my car,
That keeps me on the go.
He's the pure white filling
That fills my Oreo.

Chorus:
He's my Savior, my pride and joy,
Without his death, I'd have no life.
He's my Savior, makes my life good,
He brought me out of sin and strife.

He's my Jesus, why I want to sing,
He's why I want to shout.
He's my Jesus, I can't hold it in,
That's why I got to let it out:

Hot dog, hot dog, HOT DOG, JESUS!

Ken Casey
BEREA, KENTUCKY

"A Shotgun, a Big Plott Hound, and a Pair of Handcuffs"

THE SPORTING LIFE

Tough Birds

I had the good fortune of living with my grandfather on the farm during my first twenty years of life. Granddad was born in 1877 and died in 1960. He saw a great deal of changes in East Tennessee and was violently opposed to every one of them. He was one of the funniest people that I have ever been around. He was hardheaded. They tell me that you can always tell a Tennessean, but you can't tell them much. Granddad was one of these.

We were hunting for quail one time and flushed a covey—and if you've ever hunted quail, you know they'll scare you about half to death when you're walking along, dreaming and meditating, and suddenly six or eight will jump out from under your feet, and they sound like motorcycles when they take off. Scared us half to death. Granddad fired twice with an old two-barrel 12-gauge, and all six just kept on flying.

He looked at them for a minute, and then he turned and looked at me, then back at them, and called out, "Fly on, then, with your hearts shot out!"

Dr. Bill Foster

FLORENCE, ALABAMA

Finicky Fish

Granddad and I went fishing one time up at Dallas Bay on Chickamauga Lake. We fished all day, tried everything in the world—doughballs, shad guts—tried everything to catch fish but couldn't catch anything. Didn't get a nibble all day. Just about sundown—sunburned, hot, thirsty, tired, and we hadn't got a bite yet—Granddad finally just reached in his pocket and got a handful of change and just threw it all out into the water and said, "Here, go buy something you like!"

Dr. Bill Foster

FLORENCE, ALABAMA

Paring Down

Two liars got to bragging, and one said that he had gone ocean fishing and caught a five-hundred-pound fish.

The second one said he had been fishing out in the ocean, too. He thought he had caught a fish, but it turned out to be a lantern from the Titanic, and he said it was still lit!

The first one pondered this story for a minute and said, "Look, I'll take two hundreds pounds off that fish I caught if you'll blow out the lantern."

Margaret Rader

MCKEE, KENTUCKY

Good Prospect

A football coach from a large state university was driving in the country one day when he noticed a farm youth chasing a calf in a pasture alongside the road. He clocked him and was surprised that he was running faster than anyone he'd ever heard of. So he stopped and called to the young fellow and said, "Can you pass a football?"

The young man ambled over to the coach's car and said, "Well, I believe if I could swaller one, I could."

Pat Wagner

MOORES CREEK, KENTUCKY

High–Bridge Fishing

I woke up one day, it was the second Saturday in May, and it was so beautiful, I decided I was obligated to drive down to the Kanawa River and catch some carp. I loaded up my gear into the Great Golden Carp Cruiser, which I call G.C. for short, kissed my wife goodbye, and headed off.

I only had five dollars, so I stopped down at the local Charleston 7–11 for a can of Green Giant brand corn for the carp, a couple pieces of beef jerky, a slurpy, and since I still had a dollar left over, I bought one of those new scratch-off lottery tickets.

It was my lucky day.

I scratched off that ticket, and it was worth one thousand dollars!

Now, there were two things I could do. One was to take that money back to my wife and never see a penny of it again. Or, I could cash the ticket and spend all I wanted to and tell her I won what was left over.

I cashed that ticket quicker than a Confederate dollar at Appomattox, bought me a full tank of gas for the GC, and lit out to see Almost Heaven, West Virginia, with nine hundred eighty crisp, new one-dollar bills in my pocket.

It was a respectable wad.

I was smiling like a carp at a sewer hole in a rain storm until I hit the bridge.

There stands a bridge in Fayette County, West Virginia, which is the longest single-span arch in the world. It's the second highest in the country, and it's called the New River Gorge Bridge, and if you've never been to see it, it's well worth the trip. But if you *do* go, don't stop in the middle of that bridge for any reason.

I was about to find that out.

I was just starting across that fifteen-hundred-foot bridge when I heard an omnious sound. *Whomp, whomp, whomp.* I had me a flat tire.

I eased on the brakes and coasted to a stop right dead in the middle of that fifteen-hundred-foot bridge, right there eight hundred and seventy-six feet above the old New River.

Well, a flat's a flat, so I got out and I sweated in the hot sun. I didn't have a tire iron for the GC, so by the time I got that flat off with a pair of channel locks, I was hot, tired, and mad.

I guess I was a little bit too mad, because when I got the tire off, I flung it into the trunk, got the spare tire out and slammed it down onto the pavement. Well, that tire BOUNCED! It bounced about fourteen feet up into the air and came down about two feet away from me. Trouble was, it was two feet outside the bridge. So I stood there and watched that tire fall eight hundred and seventy-six feet down to the old New River where it bounced about three times and landed standing up in about three feet of water.

I looked seven hundred and fifty feet down to one end of the bridge and seven hundred and fifty feet to the other end of the bridge and down the gorge about a half mile, and did some quick calculating. It would take me anywhere from nine hours to two days to hike down there to get that tire, and that was if I didn't break any bones.

Then I thought about the Monster Stick.

That's my nine-foot surfcasting rod with the reel full of six miles of brand new 50-pound string carp cord. Why, I could just tie a hook to the end of that cord, snag that tire, and reel it right back to me where I stood, without ever taking a step.

I began to feel pretty good.

I tied that hook on and lowered away, and everything went pretty good for about the first four hundred and fifty feet, when the biggest redbird you ever saw swooped down, mistook that hook for a spider, snapped it up, and flew off into a rhododendron tangle. I thought about my mother and her bird feeder, and I *gently* tried to ease that bird up out of that bush, but he wouldn't budge.

Then I thought about my West Virginia state income tax return and how I'd checked the box for the non-game wildlife contribution. I said to myself, "Paul, this is the bird you bought."

I took the slack up out of the line and hauled back on the Monster Stick, and that bush just erupted into a mushroom cloud of crimson feathers and purple blossoms drifting on down toward the river, and out popped that hook and that bird and several blossoms heading right straight for my tire when lightning struck twice.

A four-foot fish mistook that blob for his fly-of-the-month subscription and paid cash on delivery. He swallowed it down, splashed into the water, swam sixteen feet, hit his head on a rock, somersaulted right through the middle of my tire, and landed up on the bank. He just laid there flopping, and I stood eight hundred and seventy-six feet above him waiting to see what would happen next.

It didn't take long.

There was a rustling in the bushes, and the biggest bear you've ever seen stepped out of the wooded area. He went up to my fish and nosed it over about three times and swallowed it. I began to feel good again, and the reason I began to feel good was because I knew there was nothing in the woods nor in the water nor in the air going to eat that bear, and I was going to get my tire back!

So I started reeling.

I reeled that bear's head right through the tire so that it settled right on his shoulders. Then I started reeling him up and was bringing him up just fine—I had just barely broke a sweat—when suddenly I heard the voice.

This was no ordinary voice.

This was the kind of voice that would wake you up in the middle of the night and tell you if you could raise eight million dollars you could go home. The voice said, "Son, what're you doing?"

I said, "Well, I'm just trying to get my tire back."

The man that belonged to the voice walked over to the edge of the bridge and looked over, and I believe it's fair to say he was a mite surprised to see what was coming up. I know *I* was surprised, because that man was a ranger. At that point, there was nothing else I could do, so I just kept on reeling and everything finally came in over the edge of the bridge.

Well, the fight had done gone out of that bear at about four hundred feet, so when he flopped down on the floor of that bridge, he just laid there. I reached for my tire.

"Freeze," said the ranger.

So I froze.

He reached into his back pocket and pulled out a notebook and reached into his front pocket and pulled out a pencil. He looked me over real hard as if he thought I was crazy and started asking me questions and writing in that book, about who was I, where was I born, where did I live, and what did I think I was doing.

He wrote for a long time, flipped a page now and then, wrote some more, then he said, "Son, I don't know why you done this. Don't want to know. I don't even know *how* you done this—but I do want you to know you're in a lot of trouble. Let's see if we understand each other, okay?"

I said, "Yes, sir."

He said, "You see that bear right there?"

I said, "Yes, sir."

He went on, "Well, that bear is a black bear. That's a state animal in the great state of West Virginia that you've taken from a no-hunting zone at a cost of five hundred dollars to yourself. That fish in that bear's mouth, that's a brook trout and is a state fish that you have taken from a no-fishing zone of the great state of West Virginia with unlawfully obtained bait, and that's a hundred dollar fine. That bird is a cardinal and is the state bird of West Virginia, non-game wildlife, which you destroyed at a cost of one hundred dollars to yourself. That flower is a rhododendron, the state flower of the great state of West Virginia, which you de-foliaged and desecrated, and that's a hundred dollar fine. And to top it all off, that tire constitutes litter you caused to be dumped into a state scenic river. Fifty dollars.

"Said fine in total shall be nine hundred fifty dollars payable in cash on the spot immediately or you'll be lawfully confined until such time that payment is made," concluded the Ranger.

He looked at me and my holey blue jeans and my worn out Army boots and rusty old G.C. tottering on three wheels, and said, "Son, you look like the kind that's gonna opt for lawful confinement, so why don't you just pack your stuff and come with me."

When I reached into my pocket, he reached for his gun. But there was no need to, because I just got out my lottery wad.

I counted him out nine hundred and fifty of those crisp new dollar bills. I put them in his hands and there was nothing he could do but to let me go. He was even so kind as to take me to a service staton owned by his brother-in-law where they fixed my flat for the amazing low price of only twenty dollars.

As I was driving back home in my G.C., I thought back to my day and decided that if every fishing trip was so expensive, I wouldn't be able to go very often.

Then I thought about my wife.

Now, my wife is the suspicious sort. I was pretty sure that if I went home and told her the story, she wasn't going to believe it. It was against my grain, but when I got home and she asked, "How'd it go?" I said, "Oh, fine, and, by the way, look what I won for you today in the lottery, sweetheart."

I pulled out those last ten new crisp one dollar bills and handed them to her.

Paul Lepp
SOUTH CHARLESTON, WEST VIRGINIA
Paul Lepp is a policeman and has won the West Virginia State Liar's Convention four times in a row.

Excessive Planning

An Englishman watching his first American football game was asked by his host what he thought about it.

"Not a bad sport," the Englishman said, "but they seem to have an excessive number of committee meetings."

Judge Ray Corns
FRANKFORT, KENTUCKY

One Catch

This fellow named Hubert Tutt was out of a job and looking, so he went to see if a friend knew about any work.

"Yes," the friend said, "Bill Plemmons down near the Smoky Mountains is an enterprising fellow. He always has some project or other going. Go see him."

So Hubert went to see Bill Plemmons and asked him if he had any work for him.

"Yes, indeed," Plemmons said. "There's big money in bears. Have you ever done any hunting?"

Hubert said he'd hunted rabbits, squirrels, and quail. Plemmons said he could probably do the job and said he would go get the equipment. He came back with a shotgun, a big Plott hound named Old Bertha, and a pair of handcuffs.

Said, "Let's go."

Hubert said, "Wait a minute. I undertstand the dog and the gun, but what are the handcuffs for?"

Plemmons said, "Oh, I forgot to tell you. There's no money in dead bears. I catch them for zoos. Live bears is where the money is, and here's how we do it. We'll go into the woods and Old Bertha will tree a bear. Now, I have the most dangerous job. I climb and shake or push the bear out of the tree. When it hits the ground, Old Bertha will come up behind him and bite him in the vital parts. Then the bear will rear up on its hind legs and go *OOH!* and grab his vitals there. That's when you put the handcuffs on him."

"Well, what's the shotgun for?" Hubert asked.

"Well, if worse should come to worst and the bear pushes me out of the tree," Plemmons said, "you shoot Old Bertha!"

Joe Kuczko

WISE, VIRGINIA

Some Duality

Members of a hunting party were asked to bring only male hounds. One guest brought a female. Out of courtesy, she was permitted to join the hunt. The pack was off in a flash and soon out of sight. The hunters asked a farmer if he had seen the hounds go by.

"Yes," he replied.

"Did you see where they went?"

"No," he replied, "but it was the first time I ever saw a fox running fifth."

Judge Ray Corns

FRANKFORT, KENTUCKY

Truthful

The facts for this story came from "Truthful" Dawkins, a farmer and fisherman, a keen student of human nature and a sort of jackleg biologist. Strange and interesting things happened to Truthful. He said one day he was crossing a swinging bridge over Elkhorn Creek, and he saw a five-pound bass about eight feet long and as big around as a milk bottle. Truthful said he killed the snake and saved the fish.

Since he had been fishing, he had some bait left and he fed some of it to the bass. For the next several days when he crossed the bridge, he would throw some bait in the same spot. The fish got so he would wait under the bridge for Truthful to feed him.

Once as he was being fed, he flopped out of the water. Truthful said he threw him back in, but from then on when Truthful showed up the fish would flop up on the bank and remain for progressively longer intervals. Soon the fish even tried to follow him, flopping about on its fins and tail.

The fish actually followed him home. Truthful fixed a tub of water for it to lounge in and it became a real pet. Soon it began to eat with the dogs and learned to growl like the mutts. One man who often "saw things" took the pledge after seeing "Fish" (as it was called) eating with the dogs.

Finally the fish got to walking so well, he followed Truthful about everywhere, and that led to tragedy. One day as they were crossing the slatted swinging bridge over Elkhorn Creek, Fish slipped between two of the slats, fell in the creek, and drowned.

John Ed McConnell
LOUISVILLE, KENTUCKY

Another Miracle

Two fellows were out duck hunting. One got to bragging about what a good shot he was and what an accurate gun he had. He said he never missed a shot and then proposed a bet that he would shoot down the first duck that flew over. Ther other hunter took him up on it. After a while a duck flew directly over them and not too high. The man cut down on him, and the duck kept on going.

"Well, I'll be darned," the man said. "We've witnessed a miracle—a dead duck flying!"

Loyal Jones

More Than Skill

Moses, Jesus, and an old man went golfing. Moses teed off, and his ball went down a waterway, the water parted, and the ball rolled across within four inches of the cup.

Jesus then teed off, and the ball hit near the water, skipped across on top of it, and came within two inches of the cup.

The old man teed off next, and the ball went crooked, hit a tree, and bounced. A squirrel picked it up and ran with it across the green. An eagle swooped down, caught the squirrel, flew high up into a thunderstorm, and got struck by lightning, which made him drop the squirrel. The squirrel dropped the ball, which hit a terrapin and rolled into the cup.

Jesus said, "Nice shot, Dad."

Loyal Jones

Wrong Player

A fellow goes into a bar with a dog and says to the bartender, "I've got a talking dog here."

The bartender says, "Is that so? What can he say?"

So the fellow says, "What is my name?" and the dog goes, "Ruff, ruff"

"That's right, my name is Ralph. How are things, Rover?"

Rover goes, "Ruff, ruff."

And Ralph says, "That's right, Rover, things are rough all over. Now tell me who was the greatest baseball player of all time?"

Rover goes, "Ruff, ruff."

Ralph says, "That's good, Rover. Babe Ruth *was* the greatest."

At this point, the bartender says, "Get out of here."

So they go outside, and Rover says to Ralph, "Should I have said Mickey Mantle?"

Peter Hille

BEREA, KENTUCKY

Gourmet

There was this fellow who lived off the land, and he poached game all year. The game wardens tried to catch him but never could. Then they noticed that the woodcocks in the area were getting scarce. They knew the poacher was the problem, but they still couldn't catch him hunting.

Finally one game warden thought he would talk to him. He said, "Look, we know you are the one killing those woodhens, but we've given up catching you. Now, I won't hold it against you, but I've always wondered how a woodcock tastes. Can you tell me?"

"Well," the fellow said, "I think they're not quite as good as a bald eagle, but they *are* better than a whooping crane."

Glenn "Buddy" Westbrook
LONDON, KENTUCKY

"It's Been Nice Playing against You, Too."

MUSIC AND MUSICIANS

The Curse of the Accordion
(By one of Chet Atkins's favorite authors, submitted here as Chet reads it in his public appearances.)

After a long immunity from the dreadful insanity that moves a man to become a musician in defiance of the will of God that he should confine himself to sawing wood, I finally fell a victim to the instrument they call the accordion. Today I hate that contrivance as fervently as any man can, but at the time I speak of, I suddenly acquired a disgusting and idolatrous affection for it. I got one of powerful capacity, and learned to play "Auld Lang Syne" on it. It seems to me, now, that I must have been gifted with a sort of *inspiration* to be enabled, in the state of ignorance in which I then was, to select out of the whole range of musical compositions the one solitary tune that sounds vilest and most distressing on the accordion. I do not suppose there is another tune in the world with which I could have inflicted so much anguish upon my race as I did with that one during my short musical career.

After I had been playing "Auld Lang Syne" about a week, I had the vanity to think I could improve the original melody, and I set about adding some little flourishes and variations to it, but with rather indifferent success, I suppose, 'cause it brought my landlady into my presence with an expression about her of being opposed to such desperate enterprises. Said she, "Do you know any other tune but that, Mr. Twain?"

I told her, meekly, that I did not.

"Well, then," said she, "stick to it just as it is; don't put any variations to it, because it's rough enough on the boarders the way it is now."

I only stayed one night at my next lodginghouse. Mrs. Smith was after me early in the morning. She said, "You can go sir; I don't want you here; I have had one of your kind before——a poor lunatic, that played the banjo and danced breakdowns, and jarred the glass all out of the windows. You kept me awake all night, and if you was to do it again, I'd take and mash that thing over your head!" I could see that this woman took no delight in music, and I moved to Mrs. Brown's.

For three nights in succession, I gave my new neighbors "Auld Lang Syne," plain and unadultered. But the very first time I tried the variations, the boarders mutinied.

I went to board at Mrs. Murphy's, an Italian lady of many excellent qualities. The very first time I struck up the variations, a haggard, care-worn, cadaverous old man walked into my room and stood beaming upon me a smile of ineffable happiness. Then he placed his hand upon my head, and, looking devoutly aloft, he said with feeling unction and in a voice trembling with emotion, "God bless you, young man. God bless you! For you have done that for me which is beyond all praise. For years, I have suffered from an incurable disease, and knowing my doom was sealed and that I must die, I have striven with all my power to resign myself to my fate, but in vain. The love of life was too strong within me. But heaven bless you, benefactor! For since I heared you play that tune and those variations, I do not want to live any longer—I am entirely resigned—I am willing to die—in fact, I am anxious to die."

And then the old man fell upon my neck and wept a flood of happy tears. I was surprised at these things; but I could not help feeling a little proud at what I had done, nor could I help giving the old gentleman a parting blast in the way of some lacerating variation as he went out the door. That doubled him up like a jack-knife, and the next time he left his bed of pain and suffering, he was in a metallic coffin.

My passion for the accordion finally spent itself and died out, and I was glad when I found myself free from its unwholesome influence. While the fever was upon me, I was a living, breathing calamity wherever I went, and desolation and disaster followed in my wake. I did incalculable harm, and inflicted untold suffering upon my race with my music. Still, I derived some little benefit from that accordion; for while I continued to practice on it, I never had to pay any board—landlords were always willing to compromise, on my leaving before the month was up.

Now, I had two objects in view in writing the foregoing, one of which was to try and reconcile people to those poor unfortunates who feel that they have a genius for music, and the other was to introduce an admirable story about little George Washington, who could not lie, and the cherry tree— or the apple tree—I have forgotten now which, although it was told me only yesterday.

Writing such a long and elaborate introductory has caused me to forget the story itself; but it was very touching.
Mark Twain, 1864

Everybody's A Critic

Back in the Old West during the mid-1800s, traveling by wagon train was pretty bad at best. They were having big trouble with the Indians. It was scary. There had been a lot of massacres.

The people on this particular train observed lots of fires and smoke in the distance, and they had seen Indians in warpaint. So that night they circled the wagons up a little tighter, built a bigger bonfire, and everybody slept with a gun and one eye open.

There were two cavalrymen watching and scouting that night just outside the circle. A coyote howled and the two men jumped, started whispering to each other about the situation. Just about that time Indian war drums started pounding. *PUM-pum-pum-pum, BOOM-boom-boom-boom.*

One cavalryman said to the other, "I don't like the sound of those drums."

A voice from the Indian side of the darkness called out softly, saying, "It's not our regular drummer!"

Bob Hannah

ATLANTA, GEORGIA

Restraint

Frank Proffitt was a wonderful traditional musician from Watauga County, North Carolina, and he played one of these small, fretless banjos that he had made himself. He had a subtle, soft, two-finger style of picking. One day, someone asked him if he could play the three-finger, Earl-Scruggs bluegrass style (which is more complicated and flashy).

He pondered this and then said, "You know, I wish I knew how to do that—and then not do it."

Loyal Jones

Competition

Back when Lester Flatt and Earl Scruggs were playing the Grand Ole Opry, fans would come backstage and ask to play with them. They would oblige their fans, although some of them were not good pickers. One night a particularly inept guitar player asked to play with Scruggs, the banjo virtuoso. They struggled through a number or two, and then the fan lavishly thanked Scruggs for the opportunity of playing with him, saying that it was one of the highlights of his life.

"It's been nice playing against you, too," Scruggs said.

Dr. Charles Wolfe

MURFREESBORO, TENNESSEE

Banjo Picker Jokes

Q: If you were in trouble and needed to send someone for help, and you had three choices, who would you send? (a) Santa Claus (b) An out-of-tune banjo picker, or (c) An in-tune banjo picker.

A: You'd send the out-of-tune banjo picker. The other two are myths.

Q: What do you say about 150,000 banjo pickers at the bottom of the ocean?

A: That's a good start.

Q: How do you get a banjo picker out of the tree?

A: Cut the rope.

Q: What's the difference between a fiddle and a banjo?

A: A banjo burns longer.

Q: What is the definition of a true gentleman?

A: A man who knows how to play the banjo, but doesn't.

Q: What's the difference between an onion and a banjo?

A: Nobody cries when you cut up a banjo.

Q: What do you say to a banjo picker in a three-piece suit?

A: Will the defendant please rise.

Q: What's the difference between a dead skunk on the road and a dead banjo picker?

A: There's skid marks in front of the skunk.

Q: What's the difference between a dead possum on the road and a dead banjo picker?

A: The possum was going to a gig.

Q: What's the difference between a trampoline and a banjo?

A: You take off your shoes to jump on a trampoline.

135

Q: What do you say about a banjo picker who is in sand up to his neck?

A: Not enough sand.

Q: What's the difference between a Harley–Davidson motorcycle and a banjo picker?

A: You can tune a Harley.

Q: If you drop a banjo and an accordion out of a plane, which hits the ground first?

A: Who cares?

Q: Why don't banjo players play hide-and-go-seek?

A: Nobody will hunt for them.

Margaret Archer

NASHVILLE, TENNESSEE

Lead singer of the group known as "The Cluster Pluckers" and married to banjo player Richard Bailey, who helped her with research.

Used Caskets

There was this fellow who was given the CB handle of "Ears" because all he would ever do was listen. He wouldn't talk, and that made him a particularly valuable driver. He drove for a well-known casket company, but he had a specific run to make, and that was picking up used caskets and delivering them back to the factory.

Now, you might wonder about used caskets. It's quite simple. When the funeral's over and the family gets up and leaves, it's an easy thing to lift the casket out of the vault, put the body in the vault, and then take the casket back into the warehouse and kind of store it until Ears can come and pick it up. Ears would get a trailer-load of used caskets, take them back to the factory, and they'd refurbish them and sell them for new.

One day, Ears had pulled into a truck stop and was walking around kicking his tires when he heard a sound inside the truck, a sort of rubbing sound. So he opened his doors and climbed up into his trailer and found the casket the sound was coming from. He lifted the lid up, and there lay a little old man with a whole stack of music in his hand. He had a pencil with a big old eraser on it, erasing those notes right off the paper. When he got the notes on a page erased, he'd throw the sheet down.

He said, "Uh...uh...who are you?"

That little old man looked up and said, "Hank. Hank Williams."

"Y-y-you're not *the* Hank Williams, are you?"

"Who else would I be?"

"W-w-w-what are you doing with that music, 'rasing all the notes off?"

"What do you think I'm doing? I'm de-composing."

John Ferguson
SONORA, KENTUCKY

"I'll Bet You Thought I Was Enjoying It"

O T H E R   P A S T I M E S   A N D
D I V E R S I O N S

Lethal Stories

I went over into Estill County to visit some people with Tom Oren who has been living in the Northeast for several years. On the way, he told me what to expect. He said, "Mitch will probably take the men out back and sit under this apple tree in some old chairs. You'll love it."

Sure enough, as soon as we got there, we just up and headed out back. There was this apple tree and five or six old chairs, and before we had a chance to sit down, Mitch was into a story, and I guess it was about the best story I ever heard. That led to another, and then another. Some happened five years ago and some fifty. I'm not sure how *true* they were, because truth, you know, is one of the first things that gets sacrificed to make a good story.

I'm hanging on every word Mitch says, but I glance at Tom, and he's got a puzzled look on his face. Every now and then, he looks around like he's hearing something or needs to make a trip to the outhouse or something.

Finally, Tom interrupts Mitch's story and says, "Mitch, this is not the same apple tree that we used to sit under and tell stories."

Mitch says, "That's right. It died about three years ago."

Tom says, "Wonder what happened to it?"

Mitch says, "Well, I guess it just heard too many lies!"

Al White

BEREA, KENTUCKY

Keeping Cool

My father was from eastern Tennessee and my mother from northern Mississippi, but this is a story that happened on the other end of the mountains, up in Vermont.

We have some close friends who spend their summers in the same town in Vermont as does Paul Newman. The lady of the family got up very early one Sunday morning to take a long walk and to go bird watching. When she got back home, it was just eight o'clock and the rest of the family was still sleeping, so she decided to run into town and gratify this craving she had for something cold and sweet by going to the bakery shop, which was also the ice cream shop, and get a double ice cream dip. She hopped into the car, drove into town, which was completely empty at this time, and parked in front of the Ice Cream and Bakery Shop.

The only other customer there was Paul Newman, sitting at the counter eating a doughnut and having coffee. She thought to herself, this is no big deal, it's his town, too, and this poor man is entitled to his privacy just like anyone else. So I'll not make a big deal out of this. I'll just go up and get my ice cream cone like he is any other person in the world.

And she did.

She nodded to Paul Newman, put her two dollars on the counter and ordered her double-dip of ice cream. And after she completed the transaction, she walked on out, got

140

to the car, and realized that she had a handful of change but no ice cream.

She thought she had just taken her change and left, so she went back inside expecting to see the ice cream cone in a little holder, or in the hand of the clerk, or something. She went over and was about to tell the clerk what happened, but glanced over at Paul Newman, who broke into this wonderfully friendly, warm grin and said, "You put it in your purse."

Michael Martin

ANN ARBOR, MICHIGAN

Wrong Choice

Brother knows this man who had some trick dogs, and he advertised them for sale. Well, a fellow came down there and asked how much the dogs were. The man said they were a hundred dollars each. The fellow said that was too much for dogs, but the man said, "You haven't seen what these dogs can do."

So, he snapped his fingers, and the first dog turned a flip and landed on his feet. He snapped his fingers again, and the second dog turned a flip and landed on the first dog's back. He snapped his fingers again, and the third dog turned a flip, landed on the second dog's back, and sang the "Wabash Cannonball."

The fellow said, "I'll take the top one."

The dog owner said, "You wouldn't want to do that. The middle one is the ventriloquist."

Minnie Pearl

NASHVILLE, TENNESSEE

Rare Bird Watching

I've got a neighbor named Leroy Hutchinson. They call him *Dugin*, and his wife, we always called her *Nene*. Well, Nene is a tee-totaler, but Dugin likes to drink a little. He went out one night and loaded up on that Union County chicken whiskey and was gone and gone. It was two o'clock, then three o'clock, and finally he came staggering in around four o'clock.

Nene said, "Where in the world have you been?"

He said, "Now, Nene, don't get excited, everything's all right. I've been out a-bird watching."

She said, "Bird watching? At two o'clock in the morning? What kind of birds you been a-watching?"

He said, "I've been a-watching a red-headed, double-breasted mattress thrasher!"

Jesse Butcher
UNION COUNTY, TENNESSEE

Uppity

An ex-coal miner from Kentucky went to Chicago to find work. He was a good-hearted fellow, but he wouldn't take anything off of anybody. He went into a bar that had a five-hundred-pound gorilla for a bouncer. The Kentuckian drank a few and got to singing some of the old murder ballads. The owner of the bar got tired of his singing and unchained the gorilla, which went over and grabbed the miner and carried him outside.

There was a great commotion out there with a lot of banging and grunting, and finally the coal miner came back in and said, "Boy, give some people a fur coat, and they think they own the place!"

Loyal Jones

The Drunk Bar Darter

This drunk happened to stagger into a restaurant where they were having a dart-throwing contest. The bartender said, "Mister, don't you want to try and win a prize here in this contest?"

He said, "Why, shore," and staggered over to throw a dart and by some miracle hit the bull's eye. So they gave him the first prize, which was a turtle, and he staggered off with it.

142

Well, a few months later, he staggered into the same bar, and they were still having dart-throwing contests. Danged if he didn't hit the bull's eye again. The bartender said, "Hey, mister, you look kinda familiar. Have you ever won a dart-throwing contest here before?"

He said, "Yes, sir, I did."

The bartender went on, "Well, we don't want to give you the same prize you won before. What did you get?"

The drunk said, "The best I can remember, seems like it was a roast beef sandwich on a *real* hard bun!"

Billy Edd Wheeler

Good Stuff

My uncle Arlo has a little bottling works. He makes a drink he calls "Summer Vacation," because about two drinks and school is out! The boys up there like to play a little game with it. About three of them will get a half a pint of it and get out behind the barn and sit around in a circle. They'll pass it around for about fifteen minutes. Then one will get up and leave, and the others have to try to guess which one it was.

Dr. Carl Hurley

LEXINGTON, KENTUCKY

It's a Tough Job But...

A man came home late rather intoxicated with a jar of moonshine in his hand. His wife was waiting at the door for him. She grabbed the jar and said, "I'm going to see what there is in this stuff that you like so much." She took two or three big swallows, lost her breath, coughed, turned red, and sputtered, "This stuff is terrible!"

Her husband gazed her into focus and said, "And all this time, I'll bet you thought I was enjoying it."

Loyal Jones

Fun in Texas

One day my friend Cletis was counting his money. He'd done pretty well on his crops that fall, and he decided he'd

143

go to Texas. So, he gets down in Ft. Worth and gets off the bus and asks, "Where's a good place to eat?"

A man said, "Why, right down the road there's a Men's Club."

Cletis didn't realize they had a swimming pool, workout room, and all of that other good stuff. He went into the restaurant and said, "Lady, I'd like to have a steak and beer."

The waitress said, "Coming right up."

She brought him a mug that was yea-big-around and about a foot tall. Cletis said, "I just wanted a mug of beer, not the whole brewery."

She said, "Mister, this is Texas. Everything is BIG in Texas."

Directly she came back with his steak, and it hung over all sides of the plate. He said, "Lady, I just wanted a steak, I didn't want the whole cow."

She said, "Mister, this is Texas and everything is BIG in Texas."

He finally got through with his meal, and he said to the waitress, "I need to use the restroom."

She said, "It's right down that hall, third door on the right."

Well, Cletis made a mistake and turned into the third door on the left, and with just one step, he fell into the swimming pool.

"Help, help!" he yelled. "Don't flush!"

Ernest Cantrell

MEMPHIS, TENNESSEE

144

"Two Bricks Shy of a Load"

NUMSKULLS AND SIMPLETONS

Aw, You Shouldn't Have

A fellow in this frontier town who was kind of dim in the thinking department was always getting into trouble. He'd steal things and insult the women and generally was a town nuisance. Some of the straight-laced town fathers decided to teach him a lesson, and they caught him and gave him a coating of tar and feathers.

As they were riding him out of town on a rail, he said, "Fellows, if it wasn't for the honor of the thing, I'd just as soon you hadn't did it."

James "Pop" Hollandsworth
ASHEVILLE, NORTH CAROLINA

If They're So Smart...

There's a little fellow named Junior who hangs out at Alley's Grocery Store. I don't know what Junior's problem is, but the boys like to tease him. They say he is two bricks shy of a load, or two pickles shy of a barrel.

To prove it, sometimes they offer Junior his choice between a nickel and a dime. He always takes the nickel, they say, because it's bigger.

One day I was there when they did that, and after Junior grabbed the nickel, Lamar and I got him off to one side and said, "Junior, those boys are making fun of you. They think you don't know the dime is worth more than the nickel. Are you grabbing the nickel because it's bigger, or what?"

He looked at Lamar and me and said, "Well, if I took the dime, they'd quit doing it!"

Bob Hannah
ATLANTA, GEORGIA

Miracle Machine

There were some country folks, a father, mother, and son, who never had been to a city, and one day they decided to go. They went into this big hotel, and while the woman was looking at all the lights, the father and son roamed around until they saw two gold doors with numbers over them. An old woman came in, pushed a button, the doors opened, she went inside, the doors closed, and the numbers over the door went 2...3...4...5 and stopped. Then they went 4...3...2...1, the doors opened and a beautiful young woman stepped out.

The son said, "Pa, did you see that?"

His father said, "Shore did, son. Go get your Ma and we'll put her in there."

Charnett Patton
ALBANY, KENTUCKY

Mistrustful

A Hoosier and a Kentuckian were fishing one night across the river from one another. They got to talking, and since they had to shout, the Kentuckian said, "Why don't you come over here, and we can fish and talk."

The Hoosier said, "I can't swim."

So the Kentuckian turned on his flashlight, which made a nice beam in the misty night, and he said, "There, you can walk across on the beam."

The Hoosier studied the situation for a minute and said, "Oh, no. You'll turn it off about the time I get halfway across."

Margaret Rader

MCKEE, KENTUCKY

Tough Fishing

We have two old boys back home who love to fish, and they wanted to do some ice fishing. They'd heard about it up in Canada, and they took off up there. The lake was frozen nicely. They stopped just before they got to the lake at a little bait shop and got all their tackle. One of them said, "We're going to need an ice pick."

So they got that, and they took off. In about two hours, one of them was back at the shop, and said, "We're going to need another dozen ice picks." Well, the fellow in the shop wanted to ask some questions, but he didn't. He sold him the picks, and the old boy left.

In about an hour, he was back. Said, "We're going to need all the ice picks you've got."

The fellow couldn't stand it any longer. "By the way," he asked, "how are you fellows doing?"

"Not very well at all," he said. "We don't even have the boat in the water yet."

Dr. Carl Hurley

LEXINGTON, KENTUCKY

Ledfords in Endless Supply

The story goes that many years ago on Shooting Creek in Clay County [North Carolina], the clan of Ledfords had become so numerous one of the old timers got thoroughly tired of the name. He told his wife to pack her clothes and they would go so far away they wouldn't ever hear of another Ledford.

He decided to go west. Arriving at a town in a distant western state, they had walked but part way up the street when the old man spied a sign on a window reading "Ledford's Cafe."

Again they boarded a train, this one headed for California. When they got off at a town in California, the old man felt he had at last reached his goal. Suddenly he turned to his wife with an exclamation of dismay and pointed to a sign reading "Ledford Manufacturing Company."

"Look a yonder, Ma," he said. "If we ain't played the fool. Here's where they make the durn Ledfords."

Margaret Walker Freel
ANDREWS, NORTH CAROLINA

Any Time...

Two salesmen were travelling out in the country late at night when their car broke down. They went to the nearest house and knocked, and a pretty widow asked them to come in. They explained their plight, and she said they wouldn't be able to get the car fixed that night, but they were welcome to spend the night. She showed them each to a bedroom, and the next morning she cooked them a nice breakfast, called the garage, and soon their car was fixed and they were on their way.

Three months later, one of them got a big official envelope, and he opened it and then called his friend and said, "When we stayed at that widow's house that night, did you fool around with her?"

The fellow said, "Well, yes."

"Did you by any chance use my name?"

The fellow hemmed and hawed but said, "Yes, I did. Do you mind?"

"Not at all," his friend said. "She just died and left me her money."

Dr. Don Hudson
BEREA, KENTUCKY

Duz Doesn't Do It

This boy came into the grocery store to buy some Duz. The grocer reminded him that his mother didn't use Duz but used Tide. They had an argument over it.

Finally, the boy came out with it. He was getting the Duz so he could wash his canary. The grocer warned him the Duz would kill the canary, but sold it to him anyway.

A few days later, the boy was back in the store, and the grocer asked him about the canary.

"The canary is dead, if you must know."

The grocer said, "I told you that you'd kill the canary washing it in Duz."

"It wasn't the Duz," the boy said. "It was the wringer."

Bill McCampbell

HUNTSVILLE, ALABAMA

I May Be Crazy, but...

This professor was driving by a mental hospital when a tire went flat. He pulled off the road, jacked up his car, took off the lug nuts and put them in a hub cap. He put on the spare, and just then a car came by too close, hit the hub cap, and threw the nuts all over a ten-acre field. Well, the professor was stumped about what to do.

One of the patients, meantime, had been watching, and he called, "Why don't you take one nut from each other wheel and put them on this one, and that will get you home."

The professor was impressed by the suggestion and did what the man suggested. Then he thanked him and said, "Why are you in there? You're not crazy."

"Oh, I'm crazy all right," the patient said. "I'm just not stupid."

Loyal Jones

Guess Who?

This rather slow small-town fellow went to Chicago and had a taxi to drive him around to see the sights. The taxi driver got to telling him jokes and riddles.

He asked, "Who has the same mother and father that I do but is not either my brother or sister?"

The fellow couldn't think of an answer. The driver said, "It's me."

The fellow thought that was a great riddle and couldn't wait to get home and pull it on his wife. When he got home, he asked, "Who has the same mother and father as me but isn't my brother or sister?"

His wife said she didn't know, and he grinned and said, "It's a taxi driver from Chicago."

Loyal Jones

Everybody Makes Mistakes

This fellow showed up with two sore ears, all scabbed-over and swollen.

"What happened to your ears?" asked a friend.

"Well, I got this wrong number while my wife was ironing, and I picked up the hot iron instead of the phone."

"But what about the other ear?"

"That happened when the darned fool called back."

Sandra Mintz

MARBLE, NORTH CAROLINA

First Class

Two fellows grew up in the mountains, and when they were grown, one of them said he was going up North to seek his fortune. The other one said he'd stay home and look after the farm and their parents. The one up North became a salesman, soon was salesmanager, and then vice president and president of the company. Before long, his business was bought out by a big company out West. In a little while, he became president of the parent company.

One day he got a call from his brother on the farm, who said, "Daddy died, and the funeral is Friday."

He said, "Oh, my goodness. I have to leave Thursday for a big merger meeting in Japan. I just can't come, but I want you to give Daddy the best funeral you can get and send the bill to me. It's the least I can do."

Well, the brother did that, and in a few weeks, the successful brother received a bill for $6,000, and he paid it. The following month, a bill for $100 came. Thinking they had forgotten something, he paid it. The next month, another bill for $100 came, and he paid that one, too. When another $100 bill arrived the third month, he called his brother and asked if he knew why he was getting these bills.

"Oh, yes," the brother said, "I think I do. See, when we got Daddy all dressed up in his old serge suit in that new casket with that polished wood and satin lining, he just didn't look right, and since you said you wanted the best, we rented him a tuxedo."

J. Richard Carleton
GEORGETOWN, KENTUCKY

Deductive Logic

These fellows who weren't too bright were on a plane from Chicago to Los Angeles, a big four-engine jet. Not long after take-off, one of the engines conked out, and the pilot came on the intercom. "Folks, we've just lost an engine, but don't worry. We have three good ones left and they'll get us to Los Angeles—but we'll be about a half hour late."

Not long after that, another engine quit, and again the pilot came through to the passengers, telling them they'd lost another engine, but not to worry. They still had two good ones and would get there—only now they would arrive about an hour late.

Another engine went out. "We've lost another one, but don't worry. We have one good engine and we'll get to Los Angeles, only now we'll be about two hours late.

These fellows had been sitting there bug-eyed all this time, but now one turned to the other and said, "If the other engine goes out, we'll be up here all day!"

Ed Ward
BLEDSOE, KENTUCKY

"Ye Must Be a Lot of Trouble to Yeselves"

CITY FOLKS, HILL PEOPLE, OLD BOYS, AND TRICKSTERS

Maybe

One day Cletis was out plowing in a field, and a city-slicker salesman was in the area. He'd heard that hill people wouldn't make a flat commitment about anything, so he decided he was going to find out if it was true or not. He was driving down the road, and he saw my friend Cletis and stopped.

This feller talked to Cletis a few minutes, then said, "You see them black cows over there? They sure are black, aren't they?"

Cletis said, "Well, on *this* side, anyhow."

Ernest Cantrell

MEMPHIS,TENNESSEE

Enough Land and a Good Truck

One day my friend Cletis was out plowing in the field when an old boy in a pickup drove up and stopped. He had

153

about four-inch heels on his boots and a twenty-gallon hat on his head. He talked to Cletis a few minutes, then asked, "How much ground you got?"

Cletis said, "I'm pretty well fixed. I got a hundred and sixty acres."

The Texan said, "Man, if I was to get in my pickup and start early one morning, I wouldn't get plum across my land 'til night."

Cletis said, "Yeah, I used to have pickup truck like that, but I got *mine* fixed."

Ernest Cantrell
MEMPHIS, TENNESSEE

Trying to Be Helpful

I remember going to a pie supper on my little mule. About halfway through the deal, I went out to check on my mule, and somebody had painted him green! So, I went back inside, and was I ever mad, and I said, "Will the man who painted my mule green stand up right now?"

This old boy stood up, and I swear he was seven feet tall, and you know what? After he stood up, his knuckles were still dragging the ground. You've seen old boys like that. He came over to me right quick and said, "I'm the man who painted your mule green, and just what do you think you're going to do about it?"

I looked up at him, and I said, "Well, buddy, the paint's dry, and he's ready for a second coat."

Larry Sledge
REEDS SPRING, MISSOURI

Real Bad and Getting Worse

There was this pessimistic, negative-thinking fellow who had a flat tire out in the country. He looked in his trunk, and there was no jack. His son had taken it or something. He said, "Oh boy, I'm stuck here all day, no telling how long. I'll never get this thing fixed."

After sitting for a while, however, he thought maybe he ought to go and see if he could borrow a jack, but he doubted if he could find anybody, or if he did, whether they'd loan him a jack.

He walked down the road a ways and saw a nice house with three or four cars parked alongside. He went up and knocked on the door.

A pleasant-looking man came to the door and said, "Yes, can I help you?"

"Well, I doubt it," the man said. "I've had a flat and need a jack to fix it, but I'm a stranger, and I don't guess you'd want to loan me a jack, even though I promise to bring it back. You probably wouldn't want to do that, me being a stranger, and you not knowing me and all. This is a *real bad* situation, and so you just *keep* your damn jack!"

Dr. Jim W. Miller

BOWLING GREEN, KENTUCKY

It's the Truth

A man was lost and went up to a farmer's house to ask directions. He saw a mean-looking dog in the yard and stopped to ask, "Does your dog bite?"

The farmer said "No."

So the man came into the yard, and the dog bit him on the leg, which upset him.

"I thought you said your dog doesn't bite."

"That's not my dog," the farmer said.

Janice Steirn

HUNTINGTON, WEST, VIRGINIA

Fast

A cabbie was driving a New Yorker through Louisville, and he pointed out the Kentucky Center for the Arts, but all the New Yorker would do was talk about how high the buildings were in New York and how fast they could build them. He said that they had built the Empire State Building in thirty-six months, and went on to tell how fast they had built other buildings. He finished by saying they could build an entire apartment building in two weeks.

About that time, they drove by the Humana Building, a prominent Louisville landmark.

"What's that?" asked the New Yorker.

"I don't know," said the cabbie. "It wasn't there when I drove by last night."

Loyal Jones

Kind Advice

A fellow got up one morning with a hangover, went to a restaurant, and said to the waitress, "Bring me a good breakfast and a few kind words."

Presently she came back and slammed a plate of bacon and eggs in front of him and started to shuffle off.

He said, "What about the kind words?"

"Don't eat the eggs," she said.

Loyal Jones

Getting Ahead

A fellow came from West Virginia to Kentucky, and he had only one shoe on. He met a Kentuckian who asked, "Did you lose a shoe?"

"No, I found one," he said.

Lt. Gov. Brereton Jones
FRANKFORT, KENTUCKY

Strange Customs

An industrial school was being established in Hindman, Kentucky. The ladies delegated to start the school were from the lowlands. The trip from the nearest railway station, at Jackson, required two days in order to reach Hindman, and the ladies were traveling in a jolting wagon over rough, dirt roads.

They stopped at a mountaineer's home the first night. The beds were in one room. The mountaineer's wife watched, with great curiousity, the ladies undress and put on their sleeping garments before retiring.

"Do ye all do this every night before ye go to bed?" she asked them.

On being told they did, she paused for several seconds, then said, "Ye must be a lot of trouble to yeselves."

The late Dr. Josiah H. Combs

FT. WORTH, TEXAS

Helpful Fellow

A woman was on a bus with her baby, and a man looked at the baby and said, "Lady, that is the ugliest baby I ever saw."

The woman started crying like her heart was broken. When the bus stopped in a small town, a young man got on, saw the woman sobbing, and went up to her and said, "Lady, don't cry so. Whatever the matter is, it couldn't be that bad. I'll tell you what I'll do, I'll get you a glass of cold water, and that'll make you feel better."

So in a few minutes, the young man was back with a glass of water and said, "See, lady, I brought you a nice glass of water. Drink that and you will feel better, and look, I brought you a banana for your monkey, too."

Ed Ward

BLEDSOE, KENTUCKY

Thief's Choice

I had stopped at Miller's Store in Haw Creek one summer day to get an RC and there was a bunch of guys on the porch of the feed, seed, and hardware side listening to a young man bragging about his new car, a Hudson Hornet. This was in the days before the Japanese invasion when the only car or truck anybody owned was a Ford or Chivlay.

The boy just went on and on about his new Hudson—it would do eighty-five wide open, etc.—and finally one old man asked if it was true what he heard about the first night when the boy had brought his new car home.

"I heerd he was so proud of that Hudson," the old man said to the other guys, "that the first night he chained the front bumper to the outhouse so nobody could steal his new car. When he went out early the next morning, somebody had cut the chain and stole the outhouse."

Joe Bly
ASHEVILLE, NORTH CAROLINA

A Dam Good Story

Folks from the mountains are familiar with the building of reservoir lakes. Sometimes little towns get buried under the water. This man told me that's exactly what happened in West Virginia when Sutton Lake was built.

A small town known as Gad used to be right there where the dam is now, he said. As they were putting this dam in, everyone that lived in Gad had the opportunity to help name the lake and dam. They had a town meeting and decided to name it Gad Lake and Gad Dam, until one old man stood up and said, "You know, I've lived here all my life. But I was thinking about my sister-in-law, Emily, down in Big Ugly near Huntington last night, and was wondering what would happen if she came up here to visit me and we went out in my boat during the hot summer and had a terrible accident. Emily can't swim a lick, you know. What would happen if she fell out of that boat and drowned? I can just see the headlines in the paper: *Big Ugly Woman Dies in Gad Dam Boating Accident.*

"Now, we don't want that, do we? So let's just name it the Sutton Dam." And they did.

Paul Lepp
SOUTH CHARLESTON, WEST VIRGINIA

Jack and the Box of Bonbons

In the town where Jack lived, there was a doctor, and he had the most beautiful daughter in town. All the boys were interested in her. It got to where the doctor couldn't even go out on his porch without stepping on a boy. His wife couldn't throw out the dishwater without splashing it on a boy. She couldn't sweep off the front walk without sweeping up a boy.

They were getting tired of it, so the doctor told everybody throughout the neighborhood that he wanted somebody very similar to himself to come calling on his daughter. Somebody who was smart, who had potential for the future, somebody who was a healer.

Before a boy could come courting his daughter he had to cure the doctor of three diseases. The first one was he couldn't remember anything. The second was he couldn't tell the truth. And the third one was he'd lost his sense of taste.

Well, Jack had two older brothers, Tom and Will, so Jack had to wait his turn.

It was Will's turn to go first.

Will waited until the doctor's family was out one day, and he went over and nailed all the windows shut. Underneath the back porch he hid a fruit jar full of colorless but not tasteless liquid (white lightning).

It was early spring, so you still had to have a bit of fire in the house but it was getting warm.

Will knocked on the door and told the doctor he had come a-calling. He walked in and said, "It's kinda cold in here," and stoked up the fire right good. The doctor was a fleshy gentleman, and it wasn't long until he began to get a little warm under his collar. Then hot under his armpits. Then he began to get a little warm in the seat of his britches. He tried to raise the windows but couldn't. He got out his hanky and began wiping his brow.

Will said, "Sir, would you like me to go get you a dipper of water?"

The doctor said, "Oh, yes, please do that, quick."

So Will ran out around the back part of the porch and reached in under there and poured out a dipperful of that colorless but not tasteless stuff and went running back in and gave it to the doctor. The doctor grabbed it up and drank it down and started to gasp.

"Ohhh, ughhhh, *cough, cough!* Will-l-l, that was water? It was good, but it wasn't water."

Will said, "Well, it looks like I've won the chance to come courting your daughter. Seems like you've got your sense of taste back."

The doctor said, "You haven't done a thing about my inability to tell the truth or improved my memory. You lose. Go on home."

It was Tom's turn next.

Even though the doctor was a little fleshy and well advanced in years, he had the reputation of being a step-husband. (That's the feller that steps *in* when the husband steps *out.)* He was popular with the ladies and was right proud of himself, being up in years like he was and all. He thought he was something.

Tom went all around the neighborhood telling everybody that the doctor had lost his ability to satisfy a woman. That cut the doctor to the quick. He was mad. He ran into Tom on the street one day and jerked him up by the collar and said, "Boy, what in the world do you mean, telling all those filthy lies about me? I was over at Sally Brown's last night, and she thought I done just fine."

Tom said, "Well, I believe I've won the right to come a-courting your daughter."

The doctor said, "I must admit you've cured my memory, and I am telling the truth, but you didn't do a thing about my sense of taste. You have to cure all three at the same time. You failed. Go on home, Tom."

Well, now it was Jack's turn.

He had no idea what he was going to do, so he went down the road walking and leaning on fences and such. He was watching a field full of sheep when suddenly he noticed that one of them began to leave an offering to fertilize the soil. Now, sheep offerings come in groups, maybe ten or twelve sort of round pieces together. Since it was early spring and the sheep had just got out to pasture from the barn where they'd been eating hay all winter, Jack thought those pieces of straw in the sheep offerings looked a little like toasted coconut.

So he ran back to his house where he got down one of his Momma's fancy candy boxes. Jack's mother was known all over as one of the finest candy makers, famous for her boiled divinity, her peanut brittle, but most especially for her chocolate coconut bonbons. She had fancy boxes she'd ordered from New York and some little fluted paper cups to go into the divided squares in them.

Jack grabbed down some of them, grabbed the sugar bowl and went to work. He had to find twelve sheep offerings of about the same size and also the same consistency. He didn't want any that were too fresh and on the runny side nor any that were hard and crusty. He wanted the ones that were firm on the outside yet a little juicy in the middle, and he wanted a matched set, with just one a little bigger than the others.

Finally Jack got things ready and went up to the doctor's house and knocked on the door. He said, "Sir, my mom has sent you a box of her award-winning chocolate coconut bonbons."

Now, the doctor just got into a twitch.

More than anything in the world he loved chocolate coconut bonbons. He took that box and held it just like you would hold a holy relic, and he carried it over to the table and set it down. Then he lifted off the lid sort of trembling, and the juices began to gurgle up in his stomach and the saliva rose in his mouth and some of it dribbled down his chin. He licked his lips and began to feel the anticipated taste of a wonderful, sweet, toasted coconut, chewy, chocolate satisfaction. He looked down at that box and picked up the big one right in the middle and squeezed it a little.

Yep, it was fresh. It was just right. He brought it to his lips and closed his eyes.

He dropped that bonbon into his mouth and chomped down on it three times before he realized that what he had in his mouth wasn't chocolate, or coconut, or bonbons.

"Whooeee, *spit-spitooee*, awrggghhh!" the doctor went. "Lord have mercy, Jack, what in the world *was* that stuff? It tasted like sheep shit!"

Jack jumped back and said, "Why in the world are you using that ugly, nasty word about my Momma's candy?"

The doctor was spitting and shaking in his boots, trying to get rid of that stuff from his mouth.

Jack said, "Well, I've won the right to come courting your daughter."

The doctor said, "How so?"

Said Jack, "It's pretty obvious you got your sense of taste back, and you must be telling the truth, because you know my Momma's good reputation for being a fine candymaker, and you wouldn't have said that stuff was bad unless it really was."

"Whoa, wait a minute," said the doctor, "you ain't done a thing about my memory loss. You've lost. Just go on home, Jack."

Jack said, "Well, if your memory's still lost, here, have another bonbon," and held out the box of candy to the doctor.

The doctor didn't say much, just sort of backed up and hollered in to his wife to come out and meet their new son-in-law.

Jack and the doctor's daughter got married, and they had a wonderful life. The last time anyone heard anything about them, they had a sheep farm down in East Tennessee, up near Townsend on the way to the Smoky Mountains.

They were raising sheep and sitting on the porch at night, rocking and eating chocolate coconut bonbons.

Mary Peterson
LOUISVILLE, TENNESSEE

The Two Old Women's Wager
This is a traditional tale.

Now, these two old women lived away up in the mountains, and they were involved in what we might call today one-upmanship. One Sunday morning, they met right on the steps of the First Baptist Church. Now, Maudie Jenkins was known as the weaver, the spinner, and the tailor of the community. She made clothes for everybody. Elvira Henry was known for being the midwife, the granny woman, the herb doctor, the healer.

These two women met there and looked at one another.

Elvira turned to Maude and said, "Well, Maude, I see you've made yourself a new dress. Want to know how I know? Well, you've got it uneven right there, and your petticoat tail's a-showing."

"Well, Elvira," Maude said, "if we're going to get tacky this morning, I could speak to you about the last church social. The meringue on your lemon pie was *flat*."

Elvira said, "Honey, if the meringue on my lemon pie was flat, it was the *only* thing about me that was!"

And Maude said, "While we're talking about flat, I might mention that your husband, Clifford, is all the time running around sick. You know you are supposed to be the healing woman of this community, and your husband is all the time running around sick. You ask him anytime, 'Clifford, how are you doing today?' and he'll say, 'I ain't never goin' to git no better.' You're supposed to be showing him off as your example, and you can see it just ain't working."

"I know it, I know it," said Elvira. "I have a lot of trouble with that man. But if we're talking about husbands in this community, listen, you're supposed to be the leader in weaving and spinning and clothesmaking, but your husband, Jess, always looks like he got dressed out of a rag bag."

"Yes," Maude says, "I've tried to make that man new sets of clothes, but all he tells me is, 'It's just now getting comfortable in the seat of the britches.' I don't know what I'm going to do with that man. He's undoubtedly the biggest fool in this neighborhood."

"Oh, no, he's not," said Elvira. "My Clifford is the biggest fool in this neighborhood!"

"You want to bet?" said Maude.

"Let's bet," Elvira said.

And right there on the steps of the church, these two old women decided they were going to bet and see which one of them could prove without a shadow of a doubt she was married to the bigger fool.

Well, over at the Henry house, Clifford came in one day, and Elvira looked at him and said, "Honey, you don't look good. You got a kinda white, pasty color in your face. Stick out your tongue."

Now, if Clifford wasn't nothing else in the world, he was obedient.

"Oh, honey, your tongue's coated. Oh, Lord, honey, I don't know what to do with you. Maybe you'd better go lay down," she said.

Being obedient, Clifford went and laid down. He laid there awhile, and he begin to think maybe he *was* feeling pretty bad, especially since she'd give him a couple of draughts and he'd been to the outhouse seventeen times during the last forty-two minutes!

He was feeling low.

And he laid there feeling lower all the time, especially when Elvira would come in and look at him so pitiful, rub a tear from her eye, and say, "Oh, my..." and shake her head.

Now, over at the Jenkins house, Jess came in, and Maude was running her hands about an inch over the top of a table, just a-going, "Awh, awh....ummmm."

Jess said, "Sugar, what are you a-doin'?"

She said, "I want you to look a-here, just look a-here."

He said, "I am. What is it?"

She said, "I was down at the settlement today, and this-here peddler came through from North Carolina, and he was selling these wool fleeces."

"He was?"

"Yeah, he was," she said, "and let me tell you, he told me that all these fleeces came from the flock of a Baptist preacher over there in North Carolina, and all his sheep were virgin sheep. This wool has special properties. If a man's been stepping out on his wife and telling her lies, he can't see this wool. What do you think of it, sugar?"

"Lord," he said, "that's the best looking stuff I've ever seen. It's just beautiful, darling. I'm so glad you bought it. Love that color. What do you plan to do with it, honey?"

"Well," she said, "Elvira Henry just pointed out last Sunday at church how you was looking right shaggy around the edges, so I bought this wool to make you a new suit of clothes."

"Oh…" said Jesse.

Well, over at the Henry household a few days later, Elvira comes in, and she looks down and says, "Clifford, honey, I'm just a-wondering what to do about you. What you got is past my learning. So, sugar, I went ahead and had your coffin made. I thought I'd have it sent over here, and I'd set right here by you, and when the time comes—I've been down in my back so bad—all I'll have to do is just take a-hold of the sheet like this and flip you over in there.

"But listen, darling, while you're still able, why don't you just get in there and lay down for me, 'cause it'll help so much when the time comes, and it won't be *long* until the laying out comes. Boo-hoo…"

So Clifford, obedient to the end, got up and laid down in the coffin.

Now, over in the Jenkins household, Maude worked day and night. She'd card that wool, and lay it out by the fireplace, you know, for the lanolin to soak into the rolls of flax and all. She'd get up early in the morning, go to her spinning wheel, and just spin and spin. When she got that done, she got her knitting needles and knitted and knitted, warped up her loom and just threw that shuttle back and forth. She worked so hard to get that suit of clothes made! All the time she would talk about how nice the material was. It was the most wonderful stuff she'd ever worked with.

Well, the more Jess looked at it, the better he liked it. He *wanted* to see that wool more than anything in the world. It got better at every glance.

The fateful day finally came over at the Henry household. Elvira walked in one day and exclaimed, "Oh, mercy, Clifford's gone. He was such a good husband. I'm going to miss ye so much! I won't get married again for at least six months."

She walked over to the closet and put on her black dress, got two silver dollars out of her pocketbook, laid them on his eyes, folded his hands across his chest, went out and got some daisies and put in his hands, and walked out sobbing.

Now, Clifford was laying there thinking. And thinking wasn't something that Clifford was good at, but in this particular set of circumstances, he was trying hard. He remembered that the Baptist preacher always said we needn't fear death, that it was sort of like walking from one room of the house to another. He also remembered that the preacher had said that when you die, the Lord gives you a new body—a *glorified* body.

He took off the silver dollars and began to look at his body, and thought, "Golly whiz, this 'un looks just like the one I've always had." Then he thought, "Well, you got to have a funeral first. After the funeral, that's when the Lord gives you a new body."

So, he put the silver dollars back on his eyes, picked up his flowers, and laid there a-waiting for his new body.

Meanwhile, over at the Jenkins household, Jess comes in and Maude says, "Oh, I'm *so* glad I got all this done. I've just heard the awfullest news. Clifford Henry has done died, and we got to go to the funeral. Come here real quick and let me get you ready."

She helped him dress in his new hand-knitted long underwear, his new hand-knitted socks, his new woven trousers, shirt and waistcoat, and jacket—even a new hand-made tie. And as he stood there in his boots, she just looked him up and down and said, "Sugar, you ain't looked that good since the night we got married. Ummm…wonderful!"

So they started off up cemetery hill where the preacher was beginning the service. "Ashes to ashes, dust to...duss...!" The preacher stared in disbelief.

Well, Jess and Maude were a-coming up over the brow of the hill, and Jess was *so* proud of his new suit of clothes. He was all rared back and just a-strutting. When he got up to the crowd, he kind of spread his legs out, put his hands behind him and began to rock back and forth.

People began to notice the break in the service, and they thought maybe the preacher was having a heavenly vision. Then they wondered if the preacher had seen a bear coming up behind them. So a few of them decided they'd take a peek. Then a couple more.

Now, this was an old mountain community, before you could get the Playboy channel on TV. People just weren't used to frontal or rearal nudity. And they began to kind of handle this situation in three different ways. One group became just intense tree-top watchers. The more religious of the crowd began to pray fervently for the family of the deceased. The other group kind of got inorderly interested in the corpse and were just sort of froze.

All this time, Clifford was a-laying there having philosophical thoughts, such as, *I've never had a true understanding of the mystery of death. I've sat at wakes and offered my condolences many times, but never before have I realized how hard it was for people to lay still that long. I will be so glad when the Lord gives me my glorified body, 'cause I'm about to die to go to the outhouse.*

One little kid back in the back began to grab a-hold of his mama's dress tail, saying "Mama, mama...." She was one of the tree-top watchers and she whispered, "Hush, child."

He persisted. "But, Mama, Mr. Jenkins is back there *buck naked!*"

About this time, Jess began to let some of those little nagging doubts he'd had surface, and he began to remember how this was the lightest-weight suit he had ever had on. It didn't chafe or itch like most new suits do, and when he

167

walked up the cemetery hill, breezes played across his body. He thought he'd better take a real intense look at the crease down his leg just to make sure…Ohhh…*NOOOO!*

He backed up against a tree, and luckily Maude had brought a great big pocketbook, so he grabbed it and held it up in front of him.

That kind of broke the spell. People fell out, some of them leaning against tombstones, some sitting on the ground, and they were whooping and hollering and a-carrying on. It got hysterical.

Finally, Clifford sat up to see what was a-going on. He looked over at Jess and said, "Jess, I reckon I'm in heaven, but your glorified body don't look a bit better than mine does."

Everybody fell down laughing. Some slid down into the grave hole and had to be pulled out. The story came out how these two women had started out to make fools of their husbands, and everyone agreed that they did a pretty good job of it. They took a vote to see which one was the winner, and the crowd was split right down the middle.

And, you know, things haven't changed much. If I took a poll today, I bet it would still be a tie. But that's really not what matters, because there is a moral to this story: A smart woman can make a fool out of any man she wants to!

Mary Peterson
LOUISVILLE, TENNESSEE

The Sweet Singer
of Sunny Tennessee

James A. Atkins
1888–1968
GOSPEL SONG COMPOSER, CHOIR DIRECTOR,
TEACHER OF VOICE, HARMONY, COMPOSITION,
PIANO, VIOLIN, AND GUITAR

James Arlie Atkins, father of guitarist Chet Atkins, left a scrapbook full of his sayings, songs, articles, and jokes. Chet brought the scrapbook by my Nashville apartment and said I could look through it. Said, "You might find something in it you can use in your new humor book."

Did I ever! The scrapbook is a treasure.

Chet told me that his father was a self-made man, mainly self-taught, but constantly striving to improve his mind and his musical skills. You can see it in the scrapbook, in articles he wrote, such as, "Will Power, Wisdom And Character," "Some Experiences of an Evangelistic Singer," "Sailing and Drifting," and "The Power of the Voice." In the latter, he wrote:

The following story illustrates…the power and influence of the tone of voice: An elderly man who could not read received a letter from his son who was sick and asking for money. He handed it to a man to read it to him, a man who had a rough, quick-spoken, crabbed voice. The man began, "Dear Father—I am sick, cannot work, send me $10.00."

169

The old man said, "Be dinged if I do, if that's the way he's going to ask for it."

He went on his way and soon met a fellow who had a smooth mellow tone of voice and asked him to read the letter to him. He began in a very kind tone, "Dear Father—I am sick, cannot work, send me $10.00."

The old man says, "Well, if that's the way he is going to ask for it, I believe I will send it."

He took the letter and went on and soon met his beloved pastor, told him of his son's illness and aroused his pastor's sympathy and gave him the letter to read also. He began reading with tears flowing and dripping from his cheeks, in a very sympathetic tone of voice, "Dear Father—I am sick, cannot work, send me $10.00." By the time he had gotten through reading it he had the old man crying, and he said, "Well, if that is the way he is going to ask for it, I'll just send him $20.00 instead."

In conclusion, let me say, whether you are a singer, a speaker, or only a conversationalist, strive to cultivate that easy-flowing, sweet-sounding, clear and distinct tone of voice, a voice that is agreeable and pleasant to the cultivated ear. Since there is none perfect but God, we cannot hope to ever reach perfection in one iota. A perfect voice, I believe, is impossible for mortal man, but those who have acquired a voice free from any imperfections, so far as man is able to class perfection, have caused Kings to bow at their feet under the sound thereof, hence the "power of voice."

Arlie Atkins' quest for knowledge is also obvious in articles and poems written by others and included in his scrapbook, long pieces like "Patrick Henry's Defense of Three Baptist Preachers in Virginia," "Favorite Songs and How They Came To Be Written," "A Practical Study of Vocal Diction," and other pieces short and long, odds and ends, news items, poems, and thoughts to live by, including some of his own, such as this one:

170

Curiosity is the mother of attention.
Attention is the mother of interest.
Interest is the mother of knowledge.
Knowledge is the mother of self confidence.
Self confidence is the mother of venture.
Venture is the mother of success.
Success is the aim, the hope and the dream of
    every being possessed with real manhood.

What I like most about Mr. Atkins's scrapbook is the sense of humor that fills its yellowed old pages and tattered binding. He typed jokes and wrote jokes out in longhand on lined paper, plain paper, church bulletins and programs, sideways, crossways, and upside down. His sense of humor is even obvious in one of the programs itself, in which he proclaims, "Prof. J.A. Atkins' band of musical entertainers will be present and give a few numbers and Mr. Atkins will display a few stunts on his 'Hand-Saw' and 'Fiddle.' ADMISSION: 15 and 25 Cents." He obviously didn't take himself too seriously, mixing his musical showmanship with stunts like playing the saw with a fiddle bow. His handwritten notes indicate that he was always on the lookout for something funny.

You have the feeling that even at the church services where Mr. Atkins did a lot of his singing, he probably gathered some humorous material when the place got to jumping. Preachers like "Parson Jack" could get right wound up on sermons listed in the program by titles like "Paw and Ma Sold Out to the Devil and the Youngerns Gone Hog Wild!"

Born in Luttrell, Tennessee, in 1888, James Arlie Atkins showed marked musical talent from early childhood. One of his promotional pieces notes that "at the age of six he could correctly sing most all the popular hymns, also play them on the violin." He achieved a certain local fame in East Tennessee (where one of his students was Roy Acuff) and in the Pine Mountain area of North Georgia.

I think Arlie would be very proud of his son's international success and acclaim, but after reading through his scrapbook, I think he would be even more appreciative of his son's great sense of humor. So now, from the scrapbook, here are some of the jokes Arlie collected:

Hard and Soft Water

A lady was asked where her son was. She replied, "If the ice is thick as he thinks it is, he's gone skating. If it ain't, he's gone swimming."

Pig Soup

A man complained to the waitress in a local restaurant, "This soup isn't fit for a pig."

Without batting an eye, she replied, "Then I'll take it back and get you some that is."

Body Reading

A writer once said, "If I can see a girl's ankle I can tell a lot about her character."

If he could see the girls of today, he could tell their entire family history!

Some Brief Hometown Observations...

...It is so dry in Kansas that cows give evaporated milk.

...I have a suit for every day in the week: one.

...Fleas are always raising their children up to go to the dogs.

...Mosquitoes are very religious: they sing over you and then prey on your body.

Two Studies in Cooperation

...A little boy was on the back porch playing sort of rough with the reluctant cat. When they got to making a right sizeable commotion, his mother heard it and yelled out at him, "Johnny, are you pulling the cat's tail?"

"No, Mama," the little boy said, "I'm just holding her tail. She's doing all the pulling."

...A man got up feeling out of sorts one morning. He stopped on the back porch, bathed his face a little, picked up his milk pail, and went to the barn lot. Old Boss was standing there chewing her cud. She looked at him, he at her. Boss said, "You look awful bad this morning."

He said, "I feel bad, too."

He stood and looked at her. He said, "Boss, I'll just be durned if I feel like milking you this morning."

Boss said, "Well, you climb on over that fence and catch hold of me and I'll jump up and down."

He Took It Sitting Down

The Farmers Union had a meeting, with speaking and refreshments. One farmer who didn't go asked another, "Did you go to the meeting last night?"

"Yeah."

"Was there many there?"

"Yeah, 'bout full."

"Did they serve eats?"

"Yeah, some of the best grub you ever ate."

"Well, how was the speaking?"

At this point the farmer tilted his head sideways, said, "Now, I'll just tell you. If I hadn't been sitting down, I'd a-felt like I's wastin' my time."

Holding Up The Train

A man out coon hunting one night was crossing the railroad tracks when he looked and saw a train coming, so he began swinging his lantern. The engineer managed to get the train stopped, looked down at the man, said, "What's the matter, buddy?"

The man smiled up at him, said, "Do you want to buy a coon skin?"

The engineer told him where to go and how hot he hoped it would be when he got there. He called the coon hunter a name that low-rated his mother, with a string of adjectives as long as from Boaz to Birmingham preceding it.

The coon hunter says, "Don't get so darned huffy about it. I haven't even caught the coon yet!"

Silence in the Amen Corner

A country preacher took for his text "If ye must sin, do it in the name of the Lord and I'll forgive ye."

He started in by saying, "Now, the first sin I'm going to preach about is stealing. You know some of you have been sneaking out to your neighbors' henhouses...and that ain't right! You been stealing chickens...and that ain't right! You been bringing them chickens home and cooking them and not giving your preacher one bite...and that ain't right!"

After every one of his that-ain't-rights, one big sister hollered "Amen!" But after the preacher moved along to other sins like snuff dipping, the sister quit hollering *Amen!* Somebody asked her why and she said, "Cause he's done quit preachin' and gone to meddlin'."

The Preacher and the Taxi Driver

Saint Peter heard a rap at the Pearly Gates, so he opened up and said, "Who are you?"

The man standing there said, "I'm Rev. So-and-so, and I've been preaching down in yonder world for thirty long years."

Saint Peter asked him, "What good deeds have you done to merit your asking entrance through the Pearly Gates?"

The preacher said, "I've visited the sick, I've helped feed the poor, and I've preached the hell out of a heap of sinners."

Just then a taxi driver walked up and entered without question. The preacher wanted to know why.

"Because," Saint Peter said, "he's scared more hell out of folks in one hour's driving than you've preached out in thirty years."

The Muttering Pig

I was drunk and in the gutter
When a pig sat down to mutter,
And a sober passerby was heard to say:
"You can tell a man who boozes
By the company he chooses,"
Then the blasted pig got up and walked away.

The Talking Dog

A ventriloquist and his little dog were traveling through the country and stopped at a farm house where the man promised the farmer he would have the dog talk some for him if he would give them something to eat.

The farmer brought out some supper for the man and some bone scraps for the little dog. As they were eating, the ventriloquist asked the dog, "How do you like your supper, Carlo?"

"Plenty bone but not much meat!" the dog replied.

The farmer was astounded, said, "What'll you take for that dog?"

The traveller said, "Oh, I couldn't part with my dog."

"I'll give you $50 for him," the farmer said.

The ventriloquist said, "What do you think, Carlo?" And Carlo spoke back to him, "Why, that other feller offered you $150, and now you'd sell me for just $50?"

"Well, I need the money bad, Carlo," the man said, and told the farmer he would take the fifty if he would give him fifty more in a month or two when he came back through. The farmer said he would, and counted out $50 for him. The man handed the farmer the string that was tied around Carlo's neck and told Carlo goodbye.

"Are you sure you're coming back?" Carlo asked him as he walked away. The traveller said yes he was. "Well," the dog said, "I'm sorry you're selling me, but I'd hate to see you get gypped. I'll not speak another word til you come back and this old fool gives you the rest of the money."

A Reason For Not Gambling

A merchant asked a farmer to gamble with him, but the farmer said, "No, I won't gamble with you for three reasons."

"What are your reasons?" the merchant inquired.

"First of all," said the farmer, "I have no money."

"Well," replied the merchant, "to hell with your other reasons!"

Decisions, Decisions

An old bachelor was walking down the street one cold snowy day when he saw a large woman approaching. Just as she met him, she slipped and fell. The street was so slick, she was unable to regain her feet, as the old bachelor ran in circles around her wringing his hands.

A man yelled to the bachelor, "Pick her up! Pick her up!"

"I would," said the bachelor, "but I don't know where to take a-hold!"

How To Handle A Ghost

A preacher travelling through the countryside stopped at a farm house and asked to spend the night. The farmer told him the best he could afford would be to give him some old quilts, and added, "There's an old house in that field down yonder, so you could sleep there. But I'll have to warn you. They tell me the house is haunted, and once the haunt appears, you can't hardly get rid of it."

The preacher said he'd chance it because he was almighty tired and in need of some good rest.

The next morning he reported to the farmer that yes, the house *was* haunted, but he got rid of the haunt without any trouble. "How'd you do that?" the farmer asked.

"When the haunt came I sang, and the haunt sang," the preacher said. "Then I prayed, and the haunt prayed. So I passed the hat for a collection and the haunt took off. I ain't seen it since."

The Fool Wasn't Talking

A little boy was considered foolish by his parents, so when they went into town to peddle some vegetables, the father said to the boy, "Now, just keep your mouth shut and folks won't know you're foolish."

While the father was inside a store, two men came along and one said to the boy, "How do you sell your beans?"

The boy said not a word.

176

"Well then, how do you sell your potatoes, son?" the other man asked, and still there was no word from the little boy.

Said one man to the other, "What's wrong with that kid?"

"He appears to be a little fool."

When the father returned the boy was crying, so he asked him what the trouble was.

The boy replied, "I didn't open my mouth, and they found it out anyhow!"

In Chains Over Music

A man who had died recently was being shown around heaven by Saint Peter. Just as they passed a row of big beautiful mansions, the newcomer noticed a man sitting by a post with a song book in his hand. He was chained to the post and was just singing away. He asked Saint Peter why the man was chained to the post.

"There's a big county singing convention down in Tennessee this weekend. If we didn't keep him chained up, he'd slip off and go."

A Sister Sizes Up The Sermon

A certain preacher was talking to one of his better-educated sisters after his sermon and asked her, "How did you like my sermon?"

"I did not like it for three reasons," she replied curtly and without any apology. "First, you read it instead of speaking it. Second, you didn't read it right. And, third, it was not fit to read in the first place!"

That's What They All Say

One of this particular church's most faithful was a lady who was very hard of hearing, but every Sunday morning she would go around shaking hands with everybody. One morning after shaking hands all around, she shook hands with the preacher and said, "I couldn't hear your sermon, but I feel like it's my duty to come to church and fill my place in the pew."

To comfort her he leaned down and said in her ear, "I'm sorry you couldn't hear the sermon, but you probably didn't miss much, anyway."

"That's what they all say," she replied.

The Barber of Sevierville

At a revival in Sevierville, Tennessee, a barber professed religion. He got 'saved.' The preacher told him that since he was a barber and got to meet a lot of people, he could do a great work for the Lord if he would talk to them about religion and salvation. When he asked how he could get into a conversation like that with his customers, the preacher said, "Just do it casually. Talk to them about their soul, ask if their house is in order, if they are prepared to die, and so on."

The first man to come in the next day wanted a shave, so the barber put a hot towel over him, talking about the weather and what-not, and then after he had lathered the man up good, he figured it was time to get down to the religion part. He grabbed up his razor, stropped it a few times, pointed it at the man, and said bluntly, "Brother, are you prepared to die?"

The man jumped up and ran out of the barber shop with the lather still on his face.

The Exodus

In a small town in South Georgia, a hunchback belonged to the church. He walked so bent over his head was only three feet above the ground. When he died they had to strap him down in the coffin to keep him lying straight.

Just as the parson began his funeral oration the strap broke from across the hunchback's chest and he bolted upright in the coffin. The parson along with the entire congregation vacated the church at once, but not quick enough to suit the parson, for he got stuck between two very large women who were both trying to get through the door at the same time.

After what seemed an eternity, the women were running away outside the church. One of them said, "Did you hear what the Pastor said after we finally broke out?"

"It seemed to me," the other replied, "that it was something like, 'Damn the church with only one door!'"

Honeymoon Prayers

A couple got married and spent their first night at the bride's home. She was a very religious girl, so she told her husband they would have to pray before going to bed, but he said, "Not me. Why, I've never prayed a single prayer in my whole life."

"I don't care," she said, "you will tonight."

So he did pray.

Next morning at the family circle he said, "I did something last night I never did before." That got everybody's attention. Then his wife said, "Yes, and if you are not good today, I'll tell everybody how awkward you were in doing it."

That's the last of the jokes that I selected from James Arlie Atkins's scrapbook. Several of them have appeared in different garb and slightly different language in other books by me and Loyal Jones— more modern trappings, but the same jokes. It's nice to discover that these ancestral versions are just as funny as their curious reincarnations.

Many jokes and certainly almost all stories and articles of early America were heavily loaded with moral applications, and these survived well into the '20s and '30s, the decades in which these were written down by Mr. Atkins. The following story was buried within a longer article Mr. Atkins thought enough of to clip and paste into his scrapbook. I present it here, with moral intact, in my own words as I recall it.

Going Over The Books

A woman started getting suspicious of her husband when he suddenly began to miss some evening meals, saying he had to work late at the office. He had never done that until recently, soon after he had hired an attractive young secretary. When she asked him what he was doing at the office so late, he always said, "Just going over the books."

One evening about supper time, she decided to pay him a visit at the office. Just as she was going to try the door, she heard noises from within telling her clearly that if she opened the door and entered just then, she was sure to find her husband and the young secretary in a compromising position.

She quietly slipped away. She thought about what she ought to do. She was certain that if she confronted her husband directly about the situation, it would destroy their marriage. She felt sure that he had never been unfaithful before, and she wanted to ensure that he never did it again. She wanted to save the marriage if she could, but she also wanted to let her husband know in some way that she knew what had been going on.

Several nights later, they were awakened by some cats outside their bedroom window, cats in the heat of courtship and being very noisy about it. Her husband sat up in bed and said, "What are those cats doing out there?"

She pretended to be only partly awake. She said, "Oh, they're just going over the books."

Her husband wasn't sure if she had talked in her sleep, if she meant anything by her remark, or what. But he was content to lie back and ponder the matter in the silence of the night and in the peaceful private places of his heart, in the full-awake brightness of his midnight mind.

Within a week, he invited his wife to the office to meet his new secretary—an elderly woman, somewhat overweight and homely, but nice, and efficient. The wife was glad she had chosen her quiet course of action. She had preserved her marriage. Her husband came home for supper on time instead of working late going over the books.

—B.E.W.

Mike Snider, of Gleason, Tennessee

A COMEDY PROFILE

I was in Nashville, Tennessee, recently and went to a benefit show for Keith McReynolds, son of Jesse McReynolds, the great mandolin player of Jim & Jesse fame. I went to hear my favorite bluegrass group, The Cluster Pluckers, along with Bill Monroe & the Bluegrass Boys, The New Coon Creek Girls, John Hartford, Charlie Louvin, and many others.

To my surprise, Mike Snider was on the show. In fact, he led off, and even though I had heard of Mike (he's one of the newest members of The Grand Old Opry), I'd never seen him work. His humor is the kind I like. He relates it to his roots, his family, his hometown, and his travels around the country playing music. It sneaks up on you.

—B.E.W.

Hi, I'm Mike Snider.

I'm from over there in Gleason, Tennessee. Some of you might not know where Gleason is...it ain't likely you'd ever go there on purpose...and one reason Gleason is not too well known is the way they fold the road maps. We kinda get lost in the crack.

I've got a friend down there, he's trying to take on the big city ways. He put him some carpet in his bathroom the other day. He liked it so well, he's fixing to get him some more and run it all the way up to the house.

One of my closest friends down there is old Virgil McNutt. He's Gleason's local veterinarian. He's also the local taxidermist. Sure enough. Old Virgil's got a sign up over his door that says, *Either way, you'll get your dog back.*

Some of you've heard me talk about my wife, Sweetie. We had what you'd call a *planned baby.* Yeah. She said, "Honey, we're gonna have a baby in eight months, so plan on it!"

Baby Talk

You know, people talk funny when they're talking to a baby. They look down and say things like, "Well-l-l, wookie-wookie-wookie, iddy bitty cutie thang. Come on, now, oochie-coochie-goochie, tickle-wickle, smile for Mommie-Nommie."

One time, Sweetie laid the baby on its back and started in talking like that and then unpinned the baby's diaper and said, "Well, looky here, what's this I found, honey? Is this a little *present* for Mommie?"

Now, if Sweetie thinks that what she found in that diaper is a present, I'm not gonnna have too much trouble finding something for her for Christmas this year!

The Neck of the House

Sweetie is awful good to me. I've been married to her for five years now, and they've been the best five years of my life. I've learned a lot of things in five years of marriage. I've learnt that a man truly is the head of the house. Course, I've also learnt that a woman is the neck, and the neck turns the head any way it wants it to go.

182

We get along real good. I don't try to run her life—and I don't try to run mine. It seems to work out better that way.

This tune we're going to do for you, here, is one that tells the story of how me and Sweetie met. It's a real romantic thing, so you might want to lean over there and gnaw on your wife's ear just a little bit.

THE SNUFF DIPPER
By Mike Snider & Malcolm Miller

Way out yonder on Grandpa's farm
Where I was born and raised,
I used to take me a moonlight stroll
In the pasture where the milkcows graze.

It was there I met this pretty little gal,
She was setting on a bobwire fence.
I grinned at her and she grinned right back
Just like she might a-had good sense.

I said, I sure am proud to meet you, ma'am,
You're just a diamond in the rough,
She said, aw, shut up that fancy talk
And give me a dip of that snuff.

I'm gonna have to admit it,
I's just a little bit surprised.
You know, when I handed her that can of snuff,
I could see love in her eyes.

Chorus:
Snuff dipper, snuff dipper,
They're the story of my life.
Snuff dipper, snuff dipper,
Now I got one for a wife.

Well, I courted that gal in the tater patch,
And I courted her in the sorghum cane.
I kissed her in the sunshine,
I even kissed her out in the rain.

183

The first time I kissed her snuff-stained lips,
We was sitting on a holler log,
And the sound rang through them mountains
Like the wail of an old coon dog.

I said, that sure was one more pucker, Sweetie,
You really know your stuff.
She said, You didn't want no kiss a-tall,
You just stole my dip of snuff.

Then one night when the time seemed right,
I said, Sweetie, we ought to get wise.
Two could dip just as cheap as one
If we get that giant economy size.

So we went up to the preacher's house,
Said, preacher, we want to get wed.
He tied the knot, said like it or not,
She's yours til you're plumb dead.

I said, let me pay you something, preacher.
Reckon a dollar would be enough?
He said, naw, Mike, just keep your money
And give me a dip of that snuff!

Well, I got me a level-headed woman now,
And she's the sweetest thing in the South,
And the reason I say she's level-headed is
Snuff runs out of both sides of her mouth.

(Chorus)

*Mike finished his song to thunderous applause at the Station Inn
there in Nashville, and while he was shaking hands getting off stage,
I went looking for a piece of paper to write some of his jokes down.
I managed to slip my name and address to him as he was leaving,
telling him I'd love to get his song. I thought I'd never hear from
him again, but as soon as I got back from Nashville, there was a
package from him waiting for me in a stack of mail.*

In the envelope were two of his cassettes, and I have listened with pleasure to him telling about...

Airports and Airplanes

It's fun playing this music. I'm awful lucky to get to go around the country and do this for a living. A couple of years ago, I got to do something I never did get to do before, and that's fly.

You know, these airports, they don't do anything to try to help the nerves of people that's scared of flying. I mean, this new airport they got out here, it's real nice, but you take an old boy that's scared of flying...you turn off of Donaldson Pike and head into the airport there, and the first thing you see is a big sign that says *TERMINAL*.

And after you get past the terminal sign and get on the airplane and get all buckled in, the first thing they start doing is preparing you for a crash...telling you about them oxygen masks, in case the cabin gets a hole in it and you lose air pressure.

Floating Seats

And then they start telling you about the floating seats you're sitting on, seats you can use for floatation, in case the airplane was to happen to fall in the water. We'as doing a show down in Little Rock, Arkansas, and got done with our show and was coming back to Nashville. Got on the airplane, they started talking 'bout the oxygen masks and the floating seat. Now, do y'all know how much water there is between Little Rock, Arkansas, and Nashville? What I wanted was a seat that would bounce up out of a cornfield!

High Class Hotels

Me and Bob here [*Bobby Clark, his mandolin player*] travel around in the winter months doing conventions—that's when the fairs and bluegrass festivals are kinda calmed down—and these conventions are high-carpet deals. They fly you around and put you up in high class hotels.

185

Now, I've only stayed in one first class hotel. That was up in Virginia. We'as up there doing a show, and later after the show, it was about three o'clock in the morning, I'as laying in bed there asleep. Boy, I was tired, and I was just a-snoring away when a knock come on the door.

It scared me. I sat up in the bed. I said, "Who is it?"

This big ol' gruff voice outside said, kinda low like, "Have you got a woman in there with you?"

I said, "No, sir!"

Well, he opened up the door and throwed one in!

Now that's a first class hotel. But I made her leave, Sweetie.

Educated Bed Bugs

"We don't always get to stay in them nice hotels like that. Lots of times when we're travelling and have to spend the night, I have to pay the bill, so we don't stay in them fancy ones. We stay in better ones than we used to, though, cause I got broke from the habit one night. We pulled in this place and I saw it on the sign: *Double rooms, $19.95.* I thought, boy, I'm gonna get out cheap here.

So I pulled in there...the office looked pretty clean, so I'as signing our name up and I noticed a bed bug crawling across the page there where I'as signing us in. I thought, now I've seen some awful smart bed bugs, but I ain't never seen one that come down to see which room I'as checking into!

I got the key and went on to the room. Got the Presidential Suite that night. Least I thought it was. It had peanut shells and jelly beans laying all over the floor.

This motel was so cheap, the smoke alarms was coin operated!

When I went to get in the shower, I had to squeeze in it. Had a little narrow door. You could just barely squeeze in it and barely squeeze out of it.

Has any of y'all ever backed out of a hot shower square into a cold doorknob? With the key still in it?

A knock come on the door, said, "It's the maid!" I said, "Lady, whatever you do, don't turn that doorknob!"

186

Running for Poke Warden

STORIES FROM
CHARLES C. CARTER

The following stories were told by the late Charles C. Carter, who was a deputy sheriff, a member of the Kentucky House of Representatives, and for twenty years county judge of Rockcastle County, Kentucky. The stories come from his written account of alleged campaign trips while running for election as "Poke Warden" of the county. We are grateful to his grandsons Sammy Ford and State Representative Danny Ford, of Mt. Vernon, Kentucky, for permission to reprint Mr. Carter's stories. Names have been changed to protect the innocent—or the guilty, as the case may be.
—L.J.

The state had passed a law saying you couldn't catch fish any way except with hook and line. It had been reported to the game warden that Uncle Jack wasn't paying much attention to the new-passed law. For that reason they sent a game warden to see if he could catch Uncle Jack.

Of course I didn't know anything about the set up when I arrived. The game warden had come to Uncle Jack's there a week before and hired in as a work hand.

The night I arrived, after supper, the little game warden asked Uncle Jack if he ever fished any, to which Uncle Jack replied yes sometimes, do you want to go fishing?

So, after a short time Uncle Jack went out to the smoke house to get a short piece of dynamite, fuse, and cap and said let's go. The river was just below the house about 100 yards, and of course I went along as I wanted to see how they were going to catch fish with dynamite. I stood on the river bank and watched them get in the boat and start for the middle of the river then Uncle Jack lighted the fuse with the dynamite attached and pitched it to the other end of the boat where the little game warden was sitting and said, there it is, do whatever you want to with it. Of course there was nothing else he could do but throw it out into the river which the little game warden did in a hurry. We had all the fish we could carry back to the house. Next morning, the little game warden left bright and early. After he was gone all Uncle Jack said was, "That little fellow thought he was mighty smart."

ཞ   ཞ   ཞ

About this time a telephone company came into the county and started to install telephones. I was at the store and post office at a place called Burr. The fellow that owned the store was Bill Owens. He'd had a telephone installed about three weeks before I was there and on this particular day it was raining and the men were loafing around the store. It being springtime, there was a lot of thunder and lightning, as well as rain.

We were sitting around the store telling tales when the telephone rang and Bill answered it. After listening he said, "Yes, he's here." There was a fellow there by the name of Bob Jarvis, and his wife was visiting her parents at East Bernstadt, which is about twenty five miles from Burr. Bob and his wife had been having quite a bit of trouble and she was wanting to talk to him, but Bob, not understanding about telephones and how you can talk to a person twenty-five miles away,

188

objected to talking to Sara in that little box as he called it, and said he didn't believe it was Sara.

Finally Bill convinced him that he could talk to her over the phone and told Bob just to put that thing to his ear and say hello at the box and Sara would answer him. He did that, and just then there was a streak of lightning and a clap of thunder that must have struck the line, because it knocked Bob clear across the room but didn't hurt him much. After he kindly come to himself, he blinked his eyes a time or two and said, "I'll be damned if it wasn't Sara alright!"

&a.   &a.   &a.

I went out on a ridge where I met a boy about 14 years old with a home-made banjo made out of a cigar box and a groundhog skin. I stopped him, talked with him a while, then got hold of the banjo, struck the strings a time or two and asked if he could pick 'er. He said, if I couldn't pick 'er, I wouldn't pack 'er. I have found out that is a good rule, if you can't do a thing, don't fool with it.

&a.   &a.   &a.

The next day I went over to the Scaffold Cane section of the county. I stopped and talked with everybody, and I heard people talking at a country store, said well, they have gone to get married. Now me being a candidate and a Kentuckian, I know enough not to inquire into other people's business.

That afternoon about four o'clock while at Bob Brock's store where there were seven or eight men and women gathered, I noticed all of them looking out the road. There I saw old man Jim Dodd and his son Bill who I knew very well coming toward the store and walking along with them was a woman 35 years old that I recognized as old man Dodd's cook or that was what I thought.

They came on to the store and Bob Brock the store keeper said, well I reckon you and Bertha got married? The old man said yep we got married. Bill wasn't saying anything and I could see that he was mad.

189

Now Bertha was about as ugly as they make them but the old man was about 70 years old, so wasn't caring much about her looks. After staying about fifteen minutes at the store, Bertha said she believed she would go on and get supper. After she started and was about 50 yards from the store the old man stood looking at her like any new married man would when Bill started to upbraid him.

The first thing he said was, well Dad you have married her and her as ugly as hell. I just don't see what you want with a woman as ugly as she is. The old man was ready for him, because he got that far away look in his eyes. He said, Ah son look how pretty she carries her hind parts.

❋ ❋ ❋

On Monday I started out campaigning again. That afternoon there was going to be a funeral at Providence church, so I went to the church and talked with some of my friends before they brought the coffin in.

We all went inside at that time. I saw the man's wife and children all down near the front which was usual at funerals. I sat just behind them.

After they sang two or three songs the preacher got up and started telling about the man's life. I found out later that this man and his wife hadn't been getting along very well. They were continually quarreling and some of his neighbors said he wouldn't work or provide for his wife and children, said he stayed drunk most of the time and was just plain no good.

A preacher will always say good things about a man when preaching his funeral. So this preacher was telling about what a wonderful man this one was and how well he provided for his family, how well he got along and how bad they would miss him in the neighborhood.

At that his wife became confused and said to her son who was about 10 years old, son slip around there and see if that is your pappy in that coffin.

&. &. &.

When I got to be [deputy] sheriff there wasn't but a few cars in the county due to the condition of the roads. We sheriffs, there were three of us, all had horses to ride in the rough country, and one car for the roads we could use it on.

I remember late one evening Bob Abney and I were coming into town in the car, me driving, when I saw a car coming with lights on and on my side of the road. I got over just as far as I could and stopped. The other car came right up to us and stopped. I got out and went around to the other car intending to bawl the fellow out that was driving.

When I got around to the other car and could see who was driving it, there stood Jess, not a very bright fellow. I said Jess you are on the wrong side of the road aren't you? He laughed big and loud and said, if I am you are too, you are on the same side. I laughed and said I guess that's right, let's be careful from now on.

You didn't have to have a license then to drive, or anything else except a car.

&. &. &.

After my term was up as sheriff, I was elected to the office of County Judge and I want to refer to some of the cases that came before me and the Circuit Court....

One case I want to tell about was a case charging Dave with being the father of a bastard child. A girl by the name of Nettie filed the charge.

After the warrant was served Dave, he got a lawyer by the name of Laney to defend him. Laney went over the case very carefully with Dave before agreeing to defend him.

Dave told him he had never had anything to do with Nettie sexually, had never been out with her at any time or place, and was not the father of her child. Laney told him that if that was the way of it, he would take his case and defend him.

Day of the trial came and after both sides announced ready, a jury was empaneled and sworn to hear the evidence.

Nettie was sworn and testified that they had been to church on Brush Creek at night time and after services were over she and Dave started to her home walking, which was about two miles from the church and that about one half mile from the church house they stopped on the side of the road and alongside of a branch and had sexual intercourse. After further questioning she said as a result she became pregnant and the boy baby was born....

All the time Nettie was testifying Dave was sitting with both elbows on his knees and his chin in his hands.

After the prosecutor finished they called Dave to the stand. Of course Laney and everybody else was expecting Dave to deny everything.

Laney said, now Dave, you heard Nettie testify you are the father of her child and that you and she had sexual intercourse on the way home from church and where it was.

Yes, Lawyer, I heard what she said.

Laney said, well Dave, go ahead and tell the jury just what happened and what you know about the case if anything.

Dave talked loud and kindly long and slow. Dave said, Lawyer, it wasn't the way Nettie told it at all, it was up the road a little farther and on the other side of the branch.

Old Laney just got up dumb founded, stuck both hands straight up, and said good bye vain world, howdy do hell.

It was hell for Dave for sixteen years, for that is how long he had to pay $60.00 a month to Nettie for the care of the child.

          ò   ò   ò

We were talking about times and things that have happened when a big yellow cat crossed the jail yard with a rat in its mouth. I said, ain't that a big cat?

Nath said, I have got two little cats just exactly alike only one is black and one is white and one is a little bigger than the other one. Bodle got up to leave and said you couldn't have cats more alike than that. ò

Humor and Healing

Relieving the Ills of Mind, Body, and Society

JOHN RAYMOND COMBS

If we could package humor—somehow put it in a box or bottle—I think the law should probably require us to say: *WARNING!* Humor may be hazardous to illness, disease, discomfort, and pain.

I have a TV ad I cut out of the paper a few months ago. A cartoon shows five doctors wearing Groucho Marx glasses, noses, and moustaches—and one doctor who looks sour and dour. It says, "Five out of six doctors recommend the Fox Sunday comedies."

Health and humor is becoming an increasingly important subject, one that is widespread. In fact, a lot of hospitals now are establishing "humor rooms." An occupational therapist in an Ohio hospital told me that her hospital had a humor room, and doctors actually prescribe time in it.

I want to trace some of the major uses of humor in British and American literature, review some of the current theories about the place of humor in therapy, and then tell you about my own experience with it

❧   ❧   ❧

Silliness is next to godliness

One of the earliest uses of humor in British literature was to relieve the seriousness of religious expression and to enhance it. If you go back to the fifteenth century mystery plays, you'll see that they contained a good deal of humor.

One widely anthologized example is *The Second Shepherd's Play*. In it, a man named Mak goes out on the hillside where a bunch of shepherds are tending sheep, and in the middle of the night when the shepherds are sleeping, he steals a sheep and takes it home to his wife, Gill. Then he slips back into the midst of the shepherds and spends the rest of the night sleeping with them, thinking they will not suspect him. He has a bit of a reputation, though, and since he and his wife fear he might be suspected, she comes up with an ingenious plan. She says, "We'll put the sheep in a cradle and pretend it's a newborn baby."

Well, sure enough, the shepherds do suspect Mak, and they come to his home. There are all kinds of jokes about how the new baby smells and what a long snout it has. Gill declares that if they're lying about stealing the sheep, why, they'll just eat the baby in the cradle. Finally, the shepherds discover that Mak is indeed the thief, and they toss him in a blanket. Then the play gets around to its serious nativity theme.

By the time of the Renaissance, comedy was being introduced into tragedy to relieve tension. We call that comic relief, of course. By the time of Shakespeare, it's clear that the principle of relieving stress through humor was alive and well understood.

Mirror, mirror

Another use of humor in literature is to place the human situation in perspective. Human beings, historically, have tried to exceed their limits. Humor lets us see ourselves as we are—lets us laugh at ourselves. It advises us not to take ourselves too seriously and to recognize that the experiences of life are relative realities. Take a look at Chaucer's *Canterbury Tales*, especially "The Wife of Bath's Tale," "The Reeve's Tale," and "The Miller's Tale." They're all quite bawdy, yet they're based on a healthy view of the human body. They speak to our earthiness, to our morality, to our humanity.

(Incidentally, my first year out of graduate school, when I was teaching a group of sophomores in a survey of British literature, I wanted them to read Chaucer in Middle English. I came up with this idea. I told them that whatever they did they should *not* read "The Miller's Tale" or "The Reeve's Tale," that they were bawdy, especially bawdy in Middle English. Well, I got a call from the library later in the day that there had been a run on Chaucer's book and that every one was checked out.)

The value of Martians

Sometimes, to help us see ourselves, it's useful to have someone come from another country or another planet. There's a whole body of foreign-visitor literature—the kind of thing where visitors might come from China or from Mars, and they look at us from a different perspective. A variation is to look at ourselves from an animal's point of view, and there is a poem from the romantic period, written by Leigh Hunt, which demonstrates this quite well. It's called "The Fish, The Man, and The Spirit." The man speaks first, and the fish will have his turn.

> *You strange, astonished-looking, angle-faced,*
> *Dreary-mouthed, gaping wretches of the sea,*
> *Gulping salt-water everlastingly,*
> *Cold-blooded, though with red your blood be graced,*
> *And mute, though dwellers in the roaring waste;*
> *And you, all shapes beside, that fishy be—*
> *Some round, some flat, some long, all devilry,*
> *Legless, unloving, infamously chaste—*

O scaly, slippery, wet, swift, staring wights,
What is't ye do? what life lead? eh, dull goggles?
How do ye vary your vile days and nights?
How pass your Sundays? Are ye still but joggles
In ceaseless wash? Still nought but gapes, and bites,
And drinks, and stares, diversified with boggles?

Now, that was the man's idea of the fish, but what is useful to us is the fish's idea of the man.

Amazing monster! that for aught I know,
With the first sight of thee didst make our race
Forever stare! Oh flat and shocking face,
Grimly divided from the breast below!
Thou that on dry land horribly dost go
With a split body and most ridiculous pace,
Prong after prong, disgracer of all grace,
Long-useless-finned, haired, upright, unwet, slow!
O breather of unbreathable sword-sharp air,
How canst exist? How bear thyself, thou dry
And dreary sloth? What particle canst share
Of the only blessed life, the watery?
I sometimes see of ye an actual pair
Go by! Linked fin by fin! most odiously.

Well, that puts us in perspective, doesn't it?

A Swift kick

A primary use of humor in literature, however, has been to offer an antidote to social illness. How many writers have tried to satirize some kind of social illness? Probably the most famous piece of satire in our language is Jonathan Swift's *A Modest Proposal*, where he offered a suggestion to help the impoverished people of Ireland. He proposed they help themselves to prosperity by raising and preparing small babies for food for the rich. Not only that, they could use the skin for gloves, and so on. It's very dark humor—there's not much that's "ha, ha, ha" about that kind of humor—but it is an antidote to social illness.

A great scene of similar purpose is where Huck Finn is with Pap Finn, who is delivering a tirade against the government. He talks about a place up in Ohio where they actually let a "mulatter" vote, and says, "the country may rot for all me. I'll never vote again as long as I live." He's really turned off, and in the very next scene, Pap Finn is so drunk he's stumbling around, stumping his toe, and cursing a bluestreak. This is another case of satire, of humor as an antidote to a deep social illness.

Back in the 1950s and 1960s, Harry Golden, who published the *North Carolina Israelite*, addressed the problem of racial injustice with books like *Only In America*, where he offered us "The Vertical Negro Plan," and several similar ones. He said that nobody objects to blacks as long as they're standing up, so you could integrate the lunch counters by taking all of the seats away.

Sit down and shut up

In 1964, I was involved in a sit-in demonstration down in Beaumont, Texas. We temporarily integrated Shelton's Restaurant until we all wound up temporarily in the klink, where, by the way, they segregated us. We asked if we could be put together. "Absolutely not! This is a segregated jail!"

The black students were from Lamar University. I was there to speak during Religious Emphasis Week and simply wound up in this situation. The black students were singing freedom songs, and somebody asked this fellow—a very distinguished-looking man, by the way—why they were singing. He said, "Well, some people sing when they can't cry."

The fact is, some people *laugh* when they can't cry, and there's therapy in laughter. It is an antidote to social illness.

197

Take me away from all this...

A great many literary artists have resorted to humor simply to take their minds off their own troubles. Take Christopher Smart, an eighteenth century poet.

Christopher Smart had every reason in the world to be sad and melancholy. He spent several years in a madhouse, and he died in a debtor's prison.

He had this problem. He was very fervent about prayer; he had an *obsession* about prayer. The problem was that he would stop people in the street and ask them to kneel down right there and pray with him. Dr. Samuel Johnson said he would just as soon pray with Kit Smart as with anyone he knew, but most people didn't feel that way about it. And yet, Smart did have a strong sense of humor. He wrote a long poem called *"Jubilate Agno"* ("Rejoice in the Lamb"). Right in the middle of this long poem, he says suddenly:

> *For I will consider my Cat Jeoffry.*
> *For he is the servant of the Living God, duly and*
> *daily serving him.*
> *For at the first glance of the glory of God in the East*
> *he worships in his own way.*
> *For is this done by wreathing his body seven times*
> *round with elegant quickness.*

I'm going to grab a few more lines here and there from this poem to show you what it's like. If you like cats, you'll like this poem.

> *For when he meets another cat he will kiss her in kindness.*
> *For when he takes his prey he plays with it to give it a*
> *chance.*
> *For one mouse in seven escapes by his dallying.*
> *For he purrs in thankfulness when God tells him he is*
> *a good cat....*
> *For he is of the tribe of Tiger....*
> *For he is a mixture of gravity and waggery....*

For the divine spirit comes about his body to sustain
it in complete cat.

And so on it goes. Maybe you think Christopher Smart was mad—he did have troubles—but I think he had a real resource in the humor of that poem.

Charles Lamb was another person with a reason to be melancholy. He worked long, hard days and did his writing at night. His older sister, Mary, in a fit of insanity, killed their mother with a butcher knife and wounded their father. She was given to fits of insanity but was a brilliant woman when she was "normal." When she had these fits, he would lead her off to the asylum, carrying a straightjacket with them, both weeping. If anyone had a reason to be ill, it was Charles Lamb. Yet, he went to his grave, as far as I know, joking and playing tricks.

A melancholic's menagerie

Lord Byron is another we could point to, a man given to melancholy and degrading habits, and yet with a sense of humor. When he went up to Cambridge University, he took a girl to keep in his room, but also a bear! Behind his house in Newstead Abbey, you'll find a huge monument to his dog. Byron was an animal lover, and my contention is that animal lovers are people with senses of humor. When the poet Shelley visited Lord Byron in Italy, he reported, "Lord Byron's establishment consists of, besides servants, ten horses, eight enormous dogs, three monkeys, five cats, an eagle, a crow, and a falcon. All these, except the horses, walk about the house, which every now and then resounds with their unarbitrated quarrels as if they were the masters of it." In a postscript to this letter to Thomas Love Peacock, Shelley wrote, "After I have sealed my letter, I find my enumeration of the animals in this Circean palace was defective. And that in a material point. I have just met on the grand staircase five peacocks, two guinea hens and an Egyptian crane. I wonder who all these animals were before they changed into all these shapes."

I think humor is one of the sanity factors of our times. I put it in a class with two other things: the ability to think metaphorically and the appreciation of music. Humor completes the triumvirate.

❧   ❧   ❧

Recent studies indicate that the mind can do a lot to heal the body. In fact, disposition of mind is *exceedingly* important in the therapeutic process.

But there are people who remain thoroughly convinced that life is an awful conspiracy directed quite personally against them. This story demonstrates what I mean by "having a set mind."

> *This man—who may have had reason for a conspiratorial view of history—went to his office one day and opened the door. He heard several accountants from the Internal Revenue Service in there talking. He thought, "Boy, this is no place for me!" (He'd been juggling his books a bit.)*
>
> *He got in his car and went home. He opened the door and heard the voices of his wife and his mistress talking. "Well," he thought, "this is no place for me either."*
>
> *So, he got in his car and drove out in the countryside and parked. He reached in his glove compartment, pulled out a .45 automatic, walked out into the middle of the field, laid the gun beside him, and thought, "Before I do myself in, I guess I ought to say a little prayer." He assumed an attitude of prayer, and about that time a bird flew over and bombarded him. The payload landed on his finger. He looked at it a moment and said, "See there, Lord, that's what I mean. They sing for other people!"*

200

Now *that* is a set mind, and *this* is one of another sort.

> *There was a man who was convinced he was dead. He just lay around on the living room sofa saying, "I'm dead. I'm not living anymore." Well, all his friends came around, trying to convince him he was still alive. They tried humor, tried to josh him out of this idea that he was dead. But he said, "No, I'm dead. No two ways about it. I'm dead. I'm gone."*
>
> *One friend decided to reason with him. So he asked, "If you cut a dead man's finger would it bleed?" The dead man thought about it for a moment, and said, "No, it would not. The blood coagulates." His friend whipped out a knife and slashed the dead man's finger, and of course, the blood came pumping out. The man looked at his bleeding finger and said, "Well, I'll be damned! Dead men do bleed!"*

The set of mind has much to do with the therapeutic process.

Pssst! Want some endorphins, buddy?

About a year ago, Kentucky Educational Television ran a series of programs on the human mind. Certain psychological states cause the brain to release endorphins, a sort of mild pain killer, which have an effect like morphine. One of the programs contended this is the basis of the placebo effect. If a person believes he has received a pain killer, that belief is enough for some people, sometimes, to release endorphins which do, in fact, kill pain. The same program reported David Livingstone to have written in his diary that once he was attacked by a lion, but during the attack, he did not feel pain or terror. This is one of the earliest acknowledgments that pain is suppressed by a life-threatening situation.

I believe pain is also suppressed by humor. There is a growing awareness of the part humor plays in the therapeutic process. On April 15, 1990, there was a big article in the *Louisville Courier-Journal* about laughing yourself well.

It reported on three or four different projects in Louisville. Cancer patients go to the Funny Farm Comedy Club on Bardstown Road to listen to humor. Part of the claim is that although there is no proof that humor cures, it does increase tolerance for pain, and it does relieve stress. The article talks about the reduction of hormones that are believed to suppress the immune system, the increase of the pulse during laughter, and the return to a below-normal pulse rate after laughter. Thus, laughter is good for the respiratory system, according to the writer, and there are other benefits, such as the lowering of blood pressure.

Even Charles Schultz has gotten into the act. In one strip, Snoopy is sitting on top of his doghouse as usual, and he says to Woodstock, "You don't feel well? Maybe you need more humor in your life. They say that looking at funny movies can cure an illness. Maybe you need something to make you laugh. How about if I tell you my favorite joke?" He starts out with, "There were these two fishermen, see, and one of them was bragging about how big a fish he caught was, and it was this big..." and when he throws his arms out to show how big the fish was, he knocks Woodstock off the doghouse. After missing Woodstock, he says, "Well, I guess he felt better and went home, but I didn't finish the joke."

Norman Cousins has done more than anyone to forward the theory of humor's healing power, although he believes, as he said in his last book, he has been widely misquoted and people have exaggerated his claims about the place of humor. He never claimed that humor could *cure* a serious illness, but he sees humor as being a metaphor for more positive emotions like love, hope, and the will to live. Humor, he says, plays a big part in healing.

Cousins had an article in the *AARP News Bulletin* in February, 1989, called "The Powers of the Mind." Several years ago, he was attacked by life-threatening collagen disease. It has to do with the connective tissue of the spine, and his was supposed to be an irreversible case. Cousins began taking megadoses of Vitamin C and using laughter for his own therapy. He watched all the Marx Brothers movies he could find, and he got nurses to read funny excerpts from books to him. This is what he said: "I made the joyous discovery that ten minutes of genuine belly laughter had an anesthetic effect and would give me at least two hours of pain-free sleep."

And, of course, he recovered. Norman Cousins worked up until the time of his death at seventy-five as a professor of humanities in medicine at UCLA School of Medicine. He wrote books, played tennis, pulled practical jokes, and told stories. He also did scientific experiments.

For instance, he was intrigued by findings that stress and depression weaken immune functions. If that's true, he reasoned, you have to believe that the opposite of depression will improve the immune system. He devised an experiment in which he put himself into a positive frame of mind by dwelling upon joyous thoughts. (So it's not just humor, but anything positive and joyous that you can think about.) Afterwards, he tested himself and found a fifty-three percent increase in eight categories of disease-fighting immune cells. He also had a doctor working with him, and they discovered that the sedimentation rate, which measures the extent of inflammation or infection in the body, was reduced by laughter.

Take two Benny Hills, and call me in the morning

I am a cancer survivor. In 1984, I had cancer and got a very poor prognosis. I was given a twenty percent chance of survival on conventional treatment. I didn't like those odds very much, so I became involved in an experimental program at Vanderbilt University, a program called MEGA-COMLA, a high-dose, high-intensity chemotherapy, which worked on me.

At that time, my wife was reading everything she could get her hands on about cancer—and about the illness in general—and she happened to pick up Norman Cousins' book *Anatomy of an Illness*. She read about the regimen of humor he had adopted for himself, and we decided that as I went through chemotherapy, I would also take strong doses of humor along the way. I was in the hospital for seventy-some days, because the protocol for this treatment is quite lengthy. We did have a ten-day furlough, and we rented every video we could find that said "comedy" or "laughter" on it. We watched humor throughout my illness. At night when they'd bring me my knock-out pill, I'd say, "Put the pill there on the table, and I'll take it after I watch"—and I'm almost ashamed to admit this—"the Benny Hill Show." It struck me as funny; it caused me to laugh heartily. Then, I'd take my knock-out pill and not know anything until next morning. When I felt like reading something, I read something funny.

And I do believe that laughter played an important part in my recovery. I want to be very clear about that. I don't say that humor healed me. I think it was a confluence of factors. I put chemicals and the medical team at the top of the list, but humor also belongs in there, and the disposition of mind— the will to live. Frankly, I would have hired a voodoo doctor if I could have found one. *Anything* I could do to get my mind going in the right direction was helpful to my body.

Somewhere along the line, I had to have a liver biopsy, and I met a liver specialist who was just full of one-liners. In fact, he kept me laughing most of the time.

When he walked into the room, I said, "How are you, Doctor? We were just talking about my liver." "Well," he said, "that's a subject close to my heart." When he inserted the biopsy needle into my liver, his comment was, "See there, that didn't hurt me a bit!"

After the procedure, he asked the nurse to check my pulse. It was 76 or 78. He said "My God, you're the coolest person I've ever seen in my life; your pulse should be at least 135 or 140 right after this procedure." Then he told the nurse to check my blood pressure, and it was 124 over 72, and he said, "My God, you're ruining my day!" slapped his kit together, and went striding out of the room.

Well, I was supposed to lie there in absolute stillness for several hours after the procedure, but it's pretty hard to lie still when you're quivering with laughter, and that's just the way that guy left me! But you know, I hardly noticed the pain that's supposed to come with a liver biopsy because he kept me laughing throughout the whole thing. There's something important there for health care professionals to learn about dealing with patients—and particularly with those in pain.

Humor cannot replace physicians, chemicals, radiation, or surgery; humor alone can not cure a serious disease. But humor—as a metaphor for a person's general disposition—does play an important role in therapy. Writers and performers have known the principle of humor as healing for centuries. Happily for us, I believe the majority of people in the medical community now recognize the principle's validity.

John Raymond Combs
is a professor of English
at Kentucky Wesleyan College,
OWENSBORO, KENTUCKY

Finding Your Own Lake Wobegon:

The Healing Power of Humor

MICHAEL R. NICHOLS

I get all kinds of introductions. I was introduced recently at a Rotary Club, and the person said, "We're glad to have Dr. Nichols here today. I've heard him speak before, and he is absolutely superfluous." I complained to Dr. Roselle, who was president of the University, and he said he was introduced once by someone saying,"We're glad to hear the latest dope from Lexington."

I hope because of what I have to say today, you will live longer, have a happier marriage, lessen your chances of heart attack, stroke, cardio-vascular disease, peptic ulcers, migraine headaches, irritable bowel syndrome....(I get kind of grandiose sometimes. A fellow walked up to me one day and said, "Doc, if you can cure me of my delusions of grandeur, I will give you eternal life.") The prescription I would write for you is to laugh long and hard and often.

ᷓ&   ᷓ&   ᷓ&

About a year ago, the University Counseling Center where I work and the department I teach in, Behavioral Science in the College of Medicine, sponsored a teleconference, beamed everywhere, on "The Healing Power of Humor." It was fascinating. Biochemists, neurophysiologists, anatomists, and endocrinologists talked about what happens to the human body when you laugh. It is all very, very positive. Measuring the immune system is a subtle, sophisticated science, but there is pretty good evidence that it really makes a difference when you laugh.

Yukking toward recovery

One of the people I enjoyed particularly was Norman Cousins. About fourteen years ago, he grabbed us by the shoulder and said, "Laughter is a legitimate topic for scientific investigation." During his own illness, he found that ten minutes of good hard belly laughter gave him two hours of pain-free sleep. In part, he was psyched up, but they also did sedimentation rates before and after the laughter episodes. Each time, the sedimentation rate dropped five points. We can hope that there is a biochemical foundation for the notion that laughter is good medicine.

Mr. Cousins was a beautiful human being. He was saying we know pretty conclusively that the negative emotions—anger, depression, irritation, frustation—can make us sick. He was also saying that the positive emotions—laughter, love, faith, commitment—can help us get well.

He described being in the hospital and just feeling terrible, when he had one of these nurses who pluralize everything. Do you know nurses like that? "How are we today?" "Have we been to the bathroom this morning?" He had had it up to the chin with this, and she came in one morning and said, "Now, I know we're going to eat a good breakfast, aren't we?" She came back in a few minutes with a specimen bottle and handed it to him and said, "It's time to give our urine specimen!" She left the room, and he got the apple juice off his breakfast tray and poured it into the specimen bottle. In a few minutes, she came back, held up the specimen bottle and said, "Oh, my, my! We're a little cloudy this morning, aren't we?" He said, "We certainly are. Let's run it through again," and he drank the juice!

A short giggliography

I used to give out a long bibliography that was long on laughter, but now I can almost narrow it down to one book. It is called *Head First: Biology of Hope* (1989), and it chronicles Dr. Cousins's ten years at the Psychoneuroimmunological Institute at UCLA Medical School. It is good science, but it is also very accessible reading and gives the major thesis for his work.

If you take on faith that laughter is good for you at emotional, psychological, and physiological levels, I want to ask a question and then try to answer it. If laughter is so good for us, how come we don't laugh more? Why do we stifle and hold back laughter?

To really understand that, we need to go back a few hundred years (because ideas do have consequences) to a notion we got from our Puritan ancestors that we should be serious and sober, keep a tight rein on the emotions, not cry, and not laugh. That's why H.L. Mencken defined Puritanism as "the nagging fear that somewhere, somehow, someone might be enjoying himself."

I think of the Puritan minister Jonathan Edwards, who wrote *Sinners in the Hands of an Angry God and* said that because of original sin, newborn babes were as "loathsome in God's sight as the most evil viper that dwells in the bowels of the earth." Think about that statement coming from a man who sired fourteen little vipers of his own!

(I myself am a Presbyterian, and we do believe in original sin. I've always thought that if you are going to sin, you ought to be original about it.)

This phenomenon has another manifestation. Ever notice that things that happen in church are funnier?

I ran home to see my mother one time, and there's this great big church on the highway with a lighted board out front, and they put mottoes out there each week for the edification of the saints. That week the motto was, "If you're done with sin, come on in." I got a little closer, and someone had written in lipstick, "But if you're not quite through, call 272-0200."

I've taught at the University of Kentucky since 1973, and sometimes I get tongue-tied when I teach, but isn't it funnier when the tongue that gets tied is in church, and particularly if that tongue is the silver one of Billy Graham?

Billy Graham was in Memphis once talking to millions of people in a football stadium, and before he got into the heart of the message, he decided he'd be a little folksy.

He said, "The people of Memphis should be complimented, because on the byways and thoroughfares of this thriving metropolis, in the last sixty days, there's not been one single traffic fertility."

Then there was the radio preacher who signed off his show by saying, "Next week our sermon topic will be 'Do You Know What Hell Is?' Tune in and hear our organist."

Have you noticed how we treat our clergy a little differently? Our back gets straighter. The beer goes underneath the coffee table. The Bible gets dusted off. The late Grady Nutt, one of the great humorists of the twentieth century, understood this. He was a Baptist minister who recognized that he was treated differently from other people. He complained once, "Ministers are cursed at times because they can't curse at times."

This little six-year-old had had a wonderful day at play and couldn't wait to tell his mother all about it, and he ran in, kicked the screen door open, started telling her what was on his heart, and he didn't notice the minister sitting in the corner. He said, "Oh, Mom, we've had the

210

greatest time down at the city dump, and I had my slingshot, and I was shooting at bottles and cans, and then I saw this old rat. So, I got me a big rock, I put it in my slingshot, and I pulled back, let fly, and I got him right between the eyes, and oh, it was wonderful..." He caught sight of the minister, and finished this way: *"...AND THEN THE LORD CALLED HIM HOME."*

This reminds me of a teacher, biggest sourpuss you ever saw. The famous psychiatrist Murray Banks often tells this story.

This teacher was writing high on the board, and one of her garters showed. She heard a snicker in the back of the room.

She said, "Young man, what is your difficulty?"

He said, "Teacher, I just saw your garter."

She said, "You take your books and leave and don't you come back here for two days."

She turned around and started writing again and heard a big laugh. She said, "Young man, what is your difficulty?"

He said, "Teacher, I just saw both of your garters."

She said, "You just take your books and don't come back to this class for two weeks."

She turned around and started writing again, dropped her eraser, bent over to pick it up. A little kid jumped up, got his books and started running out of the room. She said, "Young man, where do you think you're going?"

He said, "Teacher, I see that my schooldays are over!"

Who in this story is better adjusted, the kid or the teacher?

❀   ❀   ❀

As I talk about a sense of humor, I want to define it for you, and this is one of two take-home messages. A sense of humor, in the sense of being life-giving—that is, healing psychologically and physiologically, and not just good jokes or an inappropriate defense mechanism—a life-giving sense of humor is a way of looking at your world by means of which you take yourself and the dirty deals life sometimes hands you a whole lot less seriously. It makes this a world where it's a lot easier to accept and forgive, and that's what a lot of living is all about: accepting and forgiving ourselves and certainly others. Such a sense of humor, better than anything, puts things in perspective.

Did you ever notice that you can get a flat tire—and a week later, you can laugh? I suggest that the shorter the time between the flat tire and when you laugh, the better you're going to feel.

Let me show what it means to put things in perspective. Here is a letter that the parents of a college-freshman daughter received. Put yourself in their place.

Dear Mother and Dad,

Since I left for college I've been remiss in writing, and I'm sorry for my thoughtlessness in not having written before. I will bring you up to date now, but before you read on, please sit down. You are not to read any further unless you are sitting down.

I am getting along pretty well now. The skull fracture and concussion I got when I jumped out the window of my dormitory when it caught fire shortly after my arrival here is pretty well healed. I only spent two weeks in the hospital, and now I can see almost normally and only get those sick headaches once a day.

Fortunately, the fire in the dormitory and my jump were witnessed by an attendant at the gas station near the dorm, and he was the one that called the fire department and the ambulance. He also visited me in the hospital, and since I had nowhere to live because of the burned-out dormitory, he was kind enough to invite me to share his apartment with him. It's really a basement room, but it's kind of cute.

He is a very fine boy, and we have fallen deeply in love and are planning on getting married in the near future. We haven't set an exact date yet, but it will be before my pregnancy begins to show. Yes, Mother and Dad, I am pregnant. I know how much you are looking forward to being grandparents, and I know you will welcome the baby into your home and give it the same love and devotion and tender care you gave me when I was a child.

The reason for the delay in our marriage is that my boyfriend has a minor bacterial infection which prevents us from passing our premarital blood test, and I have carelessly caught it from him. I know tyou will welcome him into the family with open arms. He is very sweet and kind, although not terribly bright, nor educated, nor ambitious.

Now that I have brought you up to date, I want to tell you that there was no dormitory fire. I did not have a concussion or a skull fracture. I was not in a hospital. I am not pregnant. I am not engaged. I am not infected, and there is no boyfriend currently in my life. However, I am getting a D in history and an F in chemistry, and I wanted you to see those marks in proper perspective.

Your loving daughter

Laughter, it seems to me, is just about always appropriate. Rabbi Earl Grollman, who has written so sensitively and eloquently about the needs of the dying and bereaved in an extraordinary book called *When a Loved One Is Dying*, very wisely includes this little vignette. It's called "A Time to Laugh."

Dying people need lightness and smiles in their lives. People who had a good sense of humor in their lifetimes often maintain this sense of humor in their dying. Somberness won't make you or your loved one feel any better. A dying person quipped, "My situation is hopeless but not serious." Humor helped her manage feelings that were too great to deal with openly. Her future was no less menacing, but it became a little easier to bear. Laughing together is one of the ways people relate to each other. One patient said to a chaplain, "You've become so morbid and gloomy since you heard my prognosis, and you used to tell me such wonderful humorous stories. I'm the same person I was before the diagnosis. How come you are not any fun anymore?"

Humility through humor

I feel richly blessed in that my own family has never let me take myself too seriously.

I get treated very deferentially at the office—"Good morning, Doctor. How are you, Doctor?"—at least, to my face. If I get to feeling just a little bit too important, all I have to do is call home and talk to my mother for instant humility training. It is remarkable how she can put things back in perspective.

(Somebody who met my parents once said, "It's not just Michael Roy; it's *all* of them!")

I was home one day visiting my parents, and I was standing by the microwave oven.

(First I have to tell you something: I'm forty-three years old, and I just got married for the first time. Is my mother happy! She wanted me to get married. She'd say, "Michael Roy, you are forty-three years old, you are a Ph.D., your face is clearing up… when are you going to work something out?" This incident happened before I worked it out.)

So I was standing by the microwave oven which my brother and I had given them.

(I have a brother who's thirty years old. He was a surprise. Actually, he was a shock. We thought Mother had the flu—we were giving her Pepto Bismol—but it was my little brother.)

Anyway, he and I gave her this oven, trying to be a source of joy and contentment to our parents in their retirement. I was standing by the microwave oven, and I said, "Boy, I hope this doesn't make me sterile." She turned to me and asked, "How would we ever know?"

I got a Christmas card three or four years ago from a friend. She said, "I'm divorced now. Let's get together." I thought that was a swell idea because she's wonderful, bright and witty and clever, and I told my parents, and my father said, "Now Michael Roy, you be nice to her, because she's been burnt." My mother said, "That's why she wrote him. She figured his flame couldn't get too hot." My brother said, "Yeah, we think his pilot light's gone out."

(A few years ago I was dating someone, and I said, "I'm saving myself for you," and she said, "Somehow, that's not enough." I said, "Is there someone else?" She said, "There's got to be.")

See why I'm humble?

But my favorite story in the world is one I want you to hang on to. The reason it's special is that it's about my old man. My dad died two years ago. Fifteen years ago, he had a stroke, and then he lived thirteen more good years.

When he had the stroke, they called me and said, "You need to get to Louisville as fast as you can. Your father's had a stroke." So I jumped in my car and drove from Lexington to Louisville in fifty-two minutes. They let me in to see my dad, who was in intensive care. You know what a somber, frightening place that is—tubes, wires, noise, lots of medical people.

Not knowing what to say, I said the worst thing I could have: "How are you?" But bless his heart, he looked at me, and you could read his mind. He was thinking, "This is my oldest child. This boy is upset. I gotta say something to this child to make him feel better."

Sick as he was, he said, "Hey, it's OK. It's going to be OK, but would you just look at all these wires? I've never seen so many wires—all this machinery, all these wires, and they're all hooked up to me. If I fart, I'll blow up the hospital generator!" For this I drove a hundred miles an hour!

Two years ago, when he passed away, I had to pick the casket out, and I did this for him—I hope he knows about it.

I went down into this room with all of these caskets in it, and they all had their lids open. I grabbed the funeral director and said, "Oh, my God, they've all escaped!"

≈   ≈   ≈

My second message to you is that every life has episodes like these. If you look at the great humorists—not comedians but humorists—Will Rogers, Mark Twain, Garrison Keillor, and Grady Nutt—you'll notice they don't tell jokes. They just describe situations, and because of their special eyes and special ears, they see the incongruities, paradoxes, inconsistencies. Garrison Keillor's Lake Wobegon becomes a wonderful place, with real people that we love and admire and find wonderfully funny. This second take-home message is that there is a Lake Wobegon in every life if you just look for it.

We try to help people do this in psychology, in counseling. Someone comes in so sad, and I say, "I want you to do me a favor. I want you to keep a humor diary. Something funny is going to happen to you every day of this week."

"Oh, no," they say, "nothing funny ever happens to me. (*Moan, groan.*)" A week later, they say, "You won't believe it! I've got something down for every day."

I say, "I believe it. You were looking for it."

They say, "Yeah, it makes things go better, doesn't it?"

It sure does. Humor adds richness, gifts, perspective—it does a lot of good things. Your Lake Wobegon is out there.

There was a school system in Pennsylvania, and they looked for their Lake Wobegon. They found it in the excuses parents wrote for their elementary school children, parents in a rush, not always using the right word, leaving a word out here and there.

Please excuse Fred for being absent yesterday. He was
* sick and I had him shot.*
Mary was sick yesterday. Please execute her.
Please excuse Fred for being. It's his father's fault.
Please excuse Fred for being absent yesterday. He had
* diarrhea yesterday and his boots leak.*

I wish I had kept a diary over the years of all the colorful statements I've found in sophomore term papers. One student wrote that "President Abraham Lincoln signed the Emasculation Proclamation." Another wrote that the "Protestant Reformation began when Martin Luther nailed his ninety-nine feces on the church door in Wittenburg, Germany." My favorite is this one because of the zany mental image it conjures up: "With boundless energy, Theodore Roosevelt irrigated the West."

Lake Wobegon exists.

Friends in Cincinnati sent me a wonderful collection of statements from insurance reports. This my favorite. I never tire of hearing it. I don't know who wrote it, but I love this guy. This is an extraordinary human being. He knows about humor. He does not take too seriously himself or what others think of him or the dirty deal that life hands him.

I am writing in response to your letter asking for additional information. In Block No. 8 of the accident report, I put, "Trying to do the job alone," as the cause of my accident. You said in your letter that I should explain more fully, and I trust that the following details will be sufficient.

I am a bricklayer by trade. On the date of the accident, I was working alone on the roof of a new six-story building. When I completed my work, I found that I had about 500 pounds of bricks left over. Rather than carry the bricks down by hand, I decided to lower them in a barrel by using a pulley, which fortunately was attached to the side of the building at the sixth floor. Securing the rope at the ground level, I went up to the

217

roof, swung the barrel out and loaded the bricks into it. Then I went back to the ground, untied the rope, and holding it lightly to insure a slow descent of the 500 pounds of brick. You will note in Block No. 11, of the accident report, I weigh 135 pounds. Due to my surprise at being jerked off the ground so suddenly, I must have lost my presence of mind and forgot to let go of the rope. Needless to say, I proceeded at a rather rapid rate up the side of the building. In the vicinity of the third floor, I met the barrel coming down. This explains the fractured skull, and broken collar bone. Slowed only slightly, I continued my rapid ascent, not stopping until the fingers of my right hand were jammed two knuckles deep in the pulley. Fortunately, by this time I had regained my presence of mind and was able to hold tightly to the rope in spite of the excruciating pain.

At approximately the same time, however, the barrel of bricks hit the ground, and the bottom fell out of the barrel. Devoid of the weight of the bricks, the barrel weighed approximately 50 pounds. I refer you again to my weight in Block No. 11 of the accident report. As you might imagine, I began a rather rapid descent down the side of the building. In the vicinity of the third floor, I met the barrel coming up. This accounts for the two fractured ankles and lacerations of the lower body area. The encounter with the barrel slowed me enough to lessen my injuries when I fell on the pile of bricks, and fortunately only three vertebrae were cracked. I am sorry to report, however, that as I lay there on the bricks, in unbearable pain, unable to stand, unable to speak, and watching the empty barrel six stories above my head, I again lost my presence of mind and let go of the rope. The empty barrel weighed more than the rope, so it came down on me and broke both of my legs.

I hope I have furnished adequate information, and I respectfully request sick leave.

Sincerely yours, _____

Real is better

Dr. Raymond Moody wrote an excellent book, called *Laugh After Laugh,* in which he summarizes the medical evidence about laughter's importance to us psychologically, emotionally, and physiologically.

I think laughter does another thing. It helps us to be real—not the fancy put-on that we may show other folks, but the real us. And real is better.

I learned something about being real from a very special person. Tom has cerebral palsy. He walks with a stagger and he talks with a slur, but he also holds a Ph.D. from Vanderbilt University. He has the most remarkable soul and spirit and sense of humor, and boy, have I learned a lot about being real, about the futility of self-pity, and about laughter from Tom.

I have a lot of stories about Tom, but my favorite is the time I saw Tom in a Convenient Food Mart. His wife Ruth was waiting in the car with their two small children, and he was getting a loaf of bread.

For us, that's no big deal, but for Tom it's the result of discipline, practice, physical therapy, and sheer determination. His form of cerebral palsy causes involuntary muscle movement which he can't control.

So Tom gets hold of that bread, and he's going to pay for it and get out of there.

Now, being a social scientist with extensive training and experience in analysis and interpretation of the subtleties and nuances of human interaction and phenomena, I say, "Gee, Tom. It looks like Ruth sent you for a loaf of bread."

He said, "Yeah. You don't think she'd send me for eggs, do you?"

Tom is a real person: laughter helps us be real.

When I look at my life, at what keeps me from breaking easily, from having sharp edges, from needing to be carefully kept, I can identify good family, good colleagues, a good job that I enjoy, but also lots and lots of laughter—looking for my Lake Wobegon—which puts things in perspective, makes me feel better physically, rallies the will to live, and helps me be real.

Michael R. Nichols
directs the Counseling Center and
teaches in the College of Medicine
at the University of Kentucky,
LEXINGTON, KENTUCKY

LOYAL JONES, a native of North Carolina, has written articles and books on Appalachian culture. He now lives in Berea, Kentucky, where he is director of the Appalachian Center at Berea College.

BILLY EDD WHEELER, a songwriter, singer, playwright, and poet, has written songs for Judy Collins, Kenny Rogers, Johnny Cash, June Carter, and the Kingston Trio. A West Virginian by birth, he lives in Swannanoa, North Carolina.

Other books of interest
from August House Publishers, Inc.

Laughter in Appalachia

Appalachia's special brand of humor—dry, colorful, and
earthy—from Loyal Jones and Billy Edd Wheeler.
ISBN 0-87483-031-1, HB, $19.95
ISBN 0-87483-032-X, TPB, $8.95

Curing the Cross-Eyed Mule

More from Jones and Wheeler—450 Appalachian jokes,
along with essays by Roy Blount, Jr., and William Lightfoot.
ISBN 0-87483-083-4, TPB, $8.95

The Preacher Joke Book

A surprisingly reverent collection of religious humor,
poking fun less at the message than at the messengers.
ISBN 0-87483-087-7, TPB, $6.95

Cowboy Folk Humor

Jokes, tall tales, and anecdotes about cowboys,
their pranks, their foibles, and their times.
ISBN 0-87483-104-0, TPB, $9.95

A Field Guide to Southern Speech

A twenty-gauge lexicon for the duck blind, the deer stand,
the skeet shoot, the bass boat, and the backyard barbecue.
ISBN 0-87483-098-2, TPB, $6.95

Gridiron Grammar

A handbook to understanding coaches, players, officials,
Monday-morning quarterbacks, and football widows in the South.
ISBN 0-87483-158-X, TBP, $6.95

Dog Tales

Some tall, some true, all collected from the oral tradition, these stories
do justice to our beloved canine friends. Just right for reading aloud.
ISBN 0-87483-076-1, TPB, $6.95

August House Publishers, Inc.
P.O. Box 3223, Little Rock, Arkansas 72203
1-800-284-8784